YOUR KNOWLEDGE HAS VALUE

- We will publish your bachelor's and master's thesis, essays and papers

- Your own eBook and book - sold worldwide in all relevant shops

- Earn money with each sale

Upload your text at www.GRIN.com
and publish for free

Bibliographic information published by the German National Library:

The German National Library lists this publication in the National Bibliography; detailed bibliographic data are available on the Internet at http://dnb.dnb.de .

This book is copyright material and must not be copied, reproduced, transferred, distributed, leased, licensed or publicly performed or used in any way except as specifically permitted in writing by the publishers, as allowed under the terms and conditions under which it was purchased or as strictly permitted by applicable copyright law. Any unauthorized distribution or use of this text may be a direct infringement of the author s and publisher s rights and those responsible may be liable in law accordingly.

Imprint:

Copyright © 2019 GRIN Verlag
Print and binding: Books on Demand GmbH, Norderstedt Germany
ISBN: 9783346078490

This book at GRIN:

https://www.grin.com/document/510384

Rajveer Rawlin

Determinants of Profitability of Listed Commercial Banks in India

GRIN Verlag

GRIN - Your knowledge has value

Since its foundation in 1998, GRIN has specialized in publishing academic texts by students, college teachers and other academics as e-book and printed book. The website www.grin.com is an ideal platform for presenting term papers, final papers, scientific essays, dissertations and specialist books.

Visit us on the internet:

http://www.grin.com/

http://www.facebook.com/grincom

http://www.twitter.com/grin_com

DETERMINANTS OF PROFITABILITY OF LISTED COMMERCIAL BANKS IN INDIA

THESIS SUBMITTED TO BHARATHIAR UNIVERSITY IN PARTIAL FULFILLMENT OF THE REQUIREMENTS FOR THE DEGREE OF **DOCTOR OF PHILOSOPHY IN MANAGEMENT**

By
RAJVEER SAMUEL RAWLIN
Reg. No. PhD-CB-JUL2011-0532

UNDER THE GUIDANCE OF
Dr. R. SHANMUGHAM
Professor of Management (Retd.)
Bharathiar School of Management and Entrepreneur Development (BSMED)
Coimbatore - 641046

RESEARCH AND DEVELOPMENT CENTRE
BHARATHIAR UNIVERSITY, COIMBATORE – 641 046
TAMIL NADU, INDIA

JULY 2018

CERTIFICATE

This is to certify that the thesis, entitled **"DETERMINANTS OF PROFITABILITY OF LISTED COMMERCIAL BANKS IN INDIA"** submitted to the Bharathiar University, in partial fulfillment of the requirements for the award of the Degree of **DOCTOR OF PHILOSOPHY IN MANAGEMENT** is a record of original research work done by **RAJVEER SAMUEL RAWLIN** during the period **2011 to 2018** of his research in the Research and Development Centre, Bharathiar University, Coimbatore - 641 046, under my supervision and guidance and the thesis has not formed the basis for the award of any Degree / Diploma / Associateship / Fellowship or other similar title of any candidate of any university.

Date:

Signature of the Guide

Countersigned

Director
Research and Development Centre
Bharathiar University

DECLARATION

I **RAJVEER SAMUEL RAWLIN,** hereby declare that the thesis, entitled **"DETERMINANTS OF PROFITABILITY OF LISTED COMMERCIAL BANKS IN INDIA"** submitted to the Bharathiar University, in partial fulfillment of the requirements for the award of the Degree of **DOCTOR OF PHILOSOPHY IN MANAGEMENT** is a record of original research work done by me during **2011 to 2018** under the supervision and guidance of **Dr. R. SHANMUGHAM,** Professor of Management (Retd.), Bharathiar School of Management and Entrepreneur Development (BEMED), Coimbatore - 641041, and it has not formed the basis for the award of any for the award of any Degree / Diploma / Associateship / Fellowship or other similar title to any candidate of any university.

Signature of the Candidate

CERTIFICATE OF GENUINENESS OF THE PUBLICATION

This is to certify that the Ph.D. candidate **RAJVEER SAMUEL RAWLIN** working under my supervision has published a research article in the refereed journal named **MUDRA JOURNAL OF FINANCE AND ACCOUNTING** with **Vol. No 4 Issue 1** Page Nos. **58 to 69** and year of publication **2017** published by **Journal Press India**. The contents of the publication incorporate part of the results presented in his thesis

Signature of the Scholar   **Research Supervisor**

BHARATHIAR UNIVERSITY
COIMBATORE - 641 046, TAMILNADU, INDIA.
State University | Re-accredited with "A" Grade by NAAC | Ranked 14th among Indian Universities by MHRD-NIRF

CERTIFICATE OF PLAGIARISM CHECK

1	Name of the Research Scholar	RAJVEER SAMUEL RAWLIN
2	Course of study	~~M.Phil.~~, / Ph.D.,
3	Title of the Thesis / Dissertation	DETERMINANTS OF PROFITABILITY OF LISTED COMMERCIAL BANKS IN INDIA
4	Name of the Supervisor	DR. RAMASWAMY SHANMUGHAM
5	Department / Institution / Research Centre — Management	RESEARCH & DEVELOPMENT CENTRE BHARATHIAR UNIVERSITY, COIMBATORE - 641046
6	Acceptable Maximum Limit	30 %
7	% of Similarity of content Identified	09 %
8	Software Used	URKUND
9	Date of verification	26/07/2018

Report on plagiarism check, items with % of similarity is attached

Signature of the Supervisor
(Seal)

Dr. R. SHANMUGHAM Ph.D
PROFESSOR
BHARATHIAR SCHOOL OF MANAGEMENT
AND ENTREPRENEUR DEVELOPMENT
BHARATHIAR UNIVERSITY, COIMBATORE

Signature of the Scholar
Rajveer Samuel

R&D Director (BU) / Head of the Department
(Seal)
DIRECTOR
Research and Development Centre
Bharathiar University
Coimbatore - 641 046

University Librarian (BU)
University Librarian
Arignar Anna Central Library
Bharathiar University
Coimbatore - 641 046

Research Coordinator (BU)

URKUND

Urkund Analysis Result

Analysed Document: Rajveer Samuel Rawlin.docx (D40653267)
Submitted: 7/26/2018 9:52:00 AM
Submitted By: bulib_librarian@yahoo.co.in
Significance: 9 %

Sources included in the report:

CHAPTER 1.docx (D38822198)
Neha thesis final 02-08-2017.docx (D29967672)
Final Ph.D. Draft (15_October_2016).docx (D22456109)
10961322027-TS(SATHYAKALA S).pdf (D25539766)
Financial Performance Analysis of Selected Private Sector Banks in India in 21st Century.pdf (D28291297)
http://tampub.uta.fi/handle/10024/102554
http://www.aeca1.org/pub/on_line/comunicaciones_xvicongresoaeca/cd/75b.pdf
https://www.coursehero.com/file/24127529/Article-on-Pakistani-Bankpdf/
https://www.greatlakes.edu.in/herald/pdfs/sept-2017/article-2.pdf
https://pocketsense.com/calculate-profitability-ratios-banks-2634.html
http://www.raiuniversity.edu/wp-content/uploads/2017/01/COMPARATIVE-STUDY-OF-PROFITABILITY-OF-NATIONALISED-BANKS.pdf
http://article.sciencepublishinggroup.com/pdf/10.11648.j.ijebo.20170501.15.pdf
https://internationaljournalofresearch.com/2017/04/05/profitability-determinants-of-islamic-banking-in-sri-lanka/
http://www.ejbe.org/EJBE2015Vol08No16p035NARWAL-PATHNEJA.pdf
http://www.strategicjournals.com/index.php/journal/article/viewFile/124/130
https://www.quora.com/How-many-nationalised-banks-are-there-in-india
https://en.wikipedia.org/wiki/Private-sector_banks_in_India
https://www.trendrr.net/1124/largest-best-public-sector-banks-in-india-famous-top-10/
https://www.ukessays.com/essays/management/indian-public-and-private-sector-banks-management-essay.php
http://shodhganga.inflibnet.ac.in/bitstream/10603/74914/7/file%205%20chapter%203.pdf
http://www.primaxijcmr.org/wp-content/uploads/2017/02/July-December-2014.pdf

Instances where selected sources appear:

115

ACKNOWLEDGEMENT

I would like to express my sincere gratitude to my guide **Dr. R. SHANMUGHAM** for his invaluable guidance and continuous support during my Ph.D study. His guidance helped me in all aspects of research and writing of this thesis. I would like to thank my parents for their continuous prayers and guidance and my wife and daughter for their encouragement and support throughout this endeavor. I would like to thank my institute the Ramaiah Institute of Management for encouraging me and providing significant time off work to help me complete this task. In this regard I would like to thank our dean, our Academic head and all teaching and non-teaching staff of my institute for their help and support. Above all I would like to thank the Lord Almighty for his grace and mercy in helping me complete this study.

Table of Contents

INTRODUCTION 1
   1.1 Introduction 1
   1.2 Statement of the Problem 2
   1.3 Research Questions 3
   1.4 Objectives of the Study 4
   1.5 Research Methodology 4
   1.6 Scope of the Study 6
   1.7 Significance of the Study 6
   1.8 Limitations of the Study 6
   1.9 Chapter Scheme 7
   References 7
BANKING SECTOR IN INDIA – A REVIEW 8
   2.1 Origin of Banking 8
   2.2 Banking in India 9
      2.2.1 The Pre-Independence Phase 9
      2.2.2 The Post-Independence Phase 10
   2.3 Classification of Banks 16
      2.3.1 The Reserve Bank of India 17
      2.3.2 Scheduled Banks 17
      2.3.3 Unscheduled Banks 18
      2.3.4 Commercial Banks 18
      2.3.5 Co-operative Banks 21
   2.4 Function of Banks 21
      2.4.1 Primary Functions 22
      2.4.2 Secondary Functions: 24
   2.5 Key Bank Performance Measures 29
      2.5.1 The Credit Deposit Ratio 29
      2.5.2 The Investment Deposit Ratio 30

2.5.3 Other Income to Total Income Ratio 31
2.5.4 Operating Expenses to Total Income Ratio 31
2.5.5 Interest Income to Total Funds Ratio 32
2.5.6 Interest Expended to Total Funds Ratio 33
2.5.7 Net Profit to Total Funds Ratio 33
2.6 Rating Frame Work for Banks 34
    2.6.1 CAMEL Rating 34
2.7 Risks Faced by Banks 41
    2.7.1 Credit Risk 41
    2.7.2 Market Risk 42
    2.7.3 Operational Risk 42
    2.7.4 Liquidity Risk 42
    2.7.5 Business Risk 42
    2.7.6 Systemic Risk 42
2.8 Banking Regulations and Regulatory Requirements 43
    2.8.1 Cash Reserve Ratio (CRR) and Statutory Liquid Ratio (SLR) 43
    2.8.2 Basel III Norms 44
2.9 Recent Trends in Indian Banking 46
2.10 Measures of Bank Profitability 46
    2.10.1 Return on Assets (ROA) 46
    2.10.2 Return on Equity (ROE) 47
    2.10.3 Net Interest Margin (NIM) 47
2.11 Determinants of Bank Profitability 47
2.12 Current Scenario in Indian Banking 47
    2.12.1 Asset Quality 48
    2.12.2 Percentage Share in Total Credit 49
    2.12.3 Growth in Advances 50
    2.12.4 Percentage Share in Total Assets and Profits 51
2.13 Operational Definitions 52

REVIEW OF LITERATURE 53
   3.1 Studies in the Global Context 53
   3.2 Studies in the Indian Context 62
   3.3 Summary of Key Determinants of Profitability and Profitability Measures used in Select Research Studies 64
   3.4 Conclusion 67

RESEARCH METHODOLOGY 68
   4.1 Conceptual Frame Work of the Study 68
   4.2 Research Design 70
      4.2.1 Variables Selected 70
      4.2.2 Development of Working Hypothesis 75
      4.2.3 Sample Design 77
      4.2.4 Collection of Data 81
      4.2.5 Data Analysis 82
   4.3 Findings Suggestions and Conclusion 97
   4.4 Bibliography 98

ANALYSIS OF DATA 99
   5.1 Test for Normality 100
   5.2 Analysis of Key Indicators of Bank Performance 109
   5.3 Impact of Bank Size, Lending Measures and Income Measures on Bank Profitability ... 118
   5.4 Impact of Employee Productivity on Bank Profitability 137
   5.5 Impact of Capital Adequacy and Asset Quality on Bank Profitability 141
   5.6 Summary of Analysis 151
   5.7 Forecasting 152
      5.7.1 Model Fitting 152

FINDINGS AND CONCLUSION 176
   6.1 Summary 176
   6.2 Findings 176
   6.3 Implications of the Study 179
      6.3.1 Implications for Bankers 180
      6.3.2 Implications for Investors 180

    6.3.3 Implications for Regulators 180

    6.4 Scope for Future Research 181

    6.5 Conclusion 181

Bibliography

Annexures

Summary of Publications and Citations

Research Paper Publication

List of Tables

Table No	Title	Page No
Table 2.1	Chronology of Events in the Banking Sector in India in the Post-Independence Phase	11
Table 2.2	Public Sector Banks in India	18
Table 2.3	Private Sector Banks in India	20
Table 2.4	Credit Deposit Ratios of Indian Banks	30
Table 2.5	Investment Deposit Ratios of Indian Banks	30
Table 2.6	Other Income to Total Income Ratios of Indian Banks	31
Table 2.7	Operating Expenses to Total Income Ratios of Indian Banks	32
Table 2.8	Interest Income to Total Funds Ratios of Indian Banks	32
Table 2.9	Interest Expended to Total Funds Ratios of Indian Banks	33
Table 2.10	Net Profit to Total Funds Ratios of Indian Banks	34
Table 3.1	Determinants of Bank Profitability	65
Table 4.1	Sample of Public Sector Banks Chosen	78
Table 4.2	Sample of Private Sector Banks Chosen	79
Table 4.3	Data Template	81
Table 4.4	Data Analysis Techniques Used in Other Major Studies	82
Table 4.5	Variable Types and Statistical Tests	88
Table 4.6	Statistical Tests and Outcomes	88
Table 5.1	Analysis of the Return on Assets (ROA)	109
Table 5.2	Analysis of the Return on Equity (ROE)	110
Table 5.3	Analysis of the Bank Size (S)	111
Table 5.4	Capital Adequacy Ratio (CAR)	112
Table 5.5	Analysis of Business per Employee (BPE)	113
Table 5.6	Analysis of the Deposit Credit Ratio (DCR)	114
Table 5.7	Analysis of Percentage Net NPA (NNPA)	115
Table 5.8	Interest Income to Average Working Funds (IIAWF)	116
Table 5.9	Noninterest Income to Average Working Funds (NIIAWF)	117
Table 5.10	Correlation Analysis between ROA and Bank Size	119
Table 5.11	Results of Quantile Regression: Return on Assets as a Function of Bank Size	120
Table 5.12	Correlation Analysis between ROE and Bank Size	121
Table 5.13	Results of Quantile Regression: Return on Equity as a Function of Bank Size	122
Table 5.14	Correlation Analysis between ROA and the Deposit Credit Ratio	123
Table 5.15	Results of Quantile Regression: Return on Assets as a Function of the Deposit Credit Ratio	124

Table 5.16	Correlation Analysis between ROE and the Deposit Credit Ratio	125
Table 5.17	Results of Quantile Regression: Return on Equity as a Function of the Deposit Credit Ratio	126
Table 5.18	Correlation Analysis between ROA and Interest Income to Average Working Funds	128
Table 5.19	Results of Quantile Regression: Return on Assets as a Function of Interest Income to Average Working Funds	128
Table 5.20	Correlation Analysis between ROA and Noninterest Income to Average Working Funds	130
Table 5.21	Results of Quantile Regression: Return on Assets as a Function of Noninterest Income to Average Working Funds	131
Table 5.22	Correlation Analysis between ROE and Interest Income to Average Working Funds	133
Table 5.23	Results of Quantile Regression: Return on Equity as a Function of Interest Income to Average Working Funds	133
Table 5.24	Correlation Analysis between ROE and Noninterest Income to Average Working Funds	135
Table 5.25	Results of Quantile Regression: Return on Equity as a Function of Noninterest Income to Average Working Funds	136
Table 5.26	Correlation Analysis between ROA and Business per Employee	138
Table 5.27	Results of Quantile Regression: Return on Assets as a Function of Business per Employee	139
Table 5.28	Correlation Analysis between ROE and Business per Employee	140
Table 5.29	Results of Quantile Regression: Return on Equity as a Function of Business per Employee	141
Table 5.30	Correlation Analysis between ROA and the Capital Adequacy Ratio	143
Table 5.31	Results of Quantile Regression: Return on Assets as a Function of the Capital Adequacy ratio	143
Table 5.32	Correlation Analysis between ROE and the Capital Adequacy Ratio	145
Table 5.33	Results of Quantile Regression: Return on Equity as a Function of the Capital Adequacy ratio	145
Table 5.34	Correlation Analysis between ROA and Percentage Net NPA	147
Table 5.35	Results of Quantile Regression: Return on Assets as a Function of Percentage Net NPA	148
Table 5.36	Correlation Analysis between ROE and Percentage Net NPA	149
Table 5.37	Results of Quantile Regression: Return on Equity as a Function of Percentage Net NPA	150

Table 5.38	Summary of Analysis	151
Table 5.39	Results of Regression Analysis	153
Table 5.40	Results of Bi-Variate Regression Analysis	153
Table 5.41	Results of Multi-Variate Regression Analysis	154
Table 5.42	Results of Multi-Variate Regression Analysis	154
Table 5.43	Results of Multi-Variate Regression Analysis	155
Table 5.44	Results of Multi-Variate Regression Analysis	156
Table 5.45	Results of Multi-Variate Regression Analysis	157
Table 5.46	Tests for Normality of Residuals and Heteroskedasticity	158
Table 5.47	Selection of Quantile	158
Table 5.48	Results of Quantile Regression: ROA as a Function of All Independent Variables	159
Table 5.49	Results of Quantile Regression: ROA as a Function of Significant Independent Variables	160
Table 5.50	Results of Regression Analysis	161
Table 5.51	Results of Bi-Variate Regression Analysis	161
Table 5.52	Results of Multi-Variate Regression Analysis	162
Table 5.53	Tests for Normality of Residuals and Heteroskedasticity	163
Table 5.54	Selection of Quantile	163
Table 5.55	Results of Quantile Regression: ROE as a Function of All Independent Variables	164
Table 5.56	Results of Quantile Regression: ROE as a Function of Significant Independent Variables	165
Table 5.57	Forecast for ROA for the Financial Year Ending March 2016	166
Table 5.58	Forecast for ROE for the Financial Year Ending March 2016	168
Table 5.59	Forecast for ROA for the Financial Year Ending March 2017	171
Table 5.60	Forecast for ROE for the Financial Year Ending March 2017	173

List of Figures

FIGURE NO	TITLE	PAGE NO
Figure 2.1	Classification of Banks	17
Figure 2.2	Function of Banks	21
Figure 2.3	Basel III Norms	44
Figure 2.4	Quarterly Growth in Non-Performing Assets (NPA's) of Indian Banks	48
Figure 2.5	Gross NPA Levels at Top Indian Banks	49
Figure 2.6	Percentage Share in Total Credit for Different Indian Bank Groups	49
Figure 2.7	Growth in Advances for Different Indian Bank Groups	50
Figure 2.8	Percentage Share in Total Assets and Profits for Different Indian Bank Groups	51
Figure 4.1	Conceptual Framework	69
Figure 4.2	Income and Cost Components of Banks	71
Figure 4.3	Plan of Analysis	84
Figure 4.4	Binomial Distribution	85
Figure 4.5	Poisson Distribution	86
Figure 4.6	Normal Distribution	87
Figure 5.1	QQ plot of the Return on Assets (ROA)	100
Figure 5.2	QQ plot of the Return on Equity (ROE)	101
Figure 5.3	QQ plot of Bank Size	102
Figure 5.4	QQ plot of the Capital Adequacy Ratio	103
Figure 5.5	QQ plot of Business per Employee	104
Figure 5.6	QQ plot of the Deposit Credit Ratio	105
Figure 5.7	QQ plot of Percentage Net NPA	106
Figure 5.8	QQ plot of Interest Income to Average Working Funds	107
Figure 5.9	QQ plot of Noninterest Income to Average Working Funds	108
Figure 5.10	Scatter Plot of ROA versus Bank Size	119
Figure 5.11	Scatter Plot of ROE versus Bank Size	121
Figure 5.12	Scatter Plot of ROA versus the Deposit Credit Ratio	123
Figure 5.13	Scatter Plot of ROE versus the Deposit Credit Ratio	125
Figure 5.14	Scatter Plot of ROA versus Interest Income to Average Working Funds	127
Figure 5.15	Scatter Plot of ROA versus Noninterest Income to Average Working Funds	130
Figure 5.16	Scatter Plot of ROE versus Interest Income to Average Working Funds	132

Figure 5.17	Scatter Plot of ROE versus Noninterest Income to Average Working Funds	135
Figure 5.18	Scatter Plot of ROA versus Business per Employee	138
Figure 5.19	Scatter Plot of ROE versus Business per Employee	140
Figure 5.20	Scatter Plot of ROA versus the Capital Adequacy Ratio	142
Figure 5.21	Scatter Plot of ROE versus the Capital Adequacy Ratio	144
Figure 5.22	Scatter Plot of ROA versus Percentage Net NPA	147
Figure 5.23	Scatter Plot of ROE versus Percentage Net NPA	149

List of Abbreviations

No.	Abbreviation	Expansion
1	A	Asset Quality
2	AIC	Akaike Criterion
3	ANOVA	Analysis of Variance
4	APA	American Psychological Association
5	BPE	Business per Employee
6	C	Capital Adequacy
7	CAR	Capital Adequacy Ratio
8	CRR	Cash Reserve Ratio
9	DCR	Deposit Credit Ratio
10	DEA	Data Envelopment Analysis
11	E	Earnings Quality
12	EPS	Earnings per Share
13	GDP	Gross Domestic Product
14	IIAWF	Interest Income to Average Working Funds
15	L	Liquidity
16	LCR	Liquidity Coverage Ratio
17	M	Managerial Efficiency
18	MAE	Mean Absolute Error
19	MENA	Middle East and North Africa
20	NIIAWF	Noninterest Income to Average Working Funds
21	NIM	Net Interest Margin
22	NNPA	Percentage Net Non-Performing Assets
23	NPA	Non-Performing Assets
24	OLS	Ordinary Least Squares
25	PAT	Profit After Tax
26	PCB	Private Commercial Banks

27	RBI	Reserve Bank of India
28	RMSE	Root Mean Squared Error
29	ROA	Return on Assets
30	ROAA	Return on Average Assets
31	ROAE	Return on Average Equity
32	ROC	Return on Capital
33	ROE	Return on Equity
34	RRB	Regional Rural Banks
35	S	Bank Size
36	SBI	State Bank of India
37	SLR	Statutory Liquid Ratio
38	VIF	Variance Inflation Factor

CHAPTER 1

INTRODUCTION

CHAPTER I

INTRODUCTION

1.1 Introduction

The reforms in the Indian banking sector have redefined the entire Indian banking landscape. The Narasimham Committee reforms in 1991 facilitated the flow of credit across all segments of the economy, deregulation of interest rates and reduction of cash reserve ratio (CRR) and statutory liquid ratio (SLR) requirements that enabled banks to be well capitalized. These reforms came along with the introduction of effective risk management practices that have made the Indian banking sector financially sound and globally competitive. These reforms were instrumental in making the Indian banking sector resilient even in the face of unprecedented global turmoil such as the global financial crisis of 2008 when a number of global financial institutions were on the verge of insolvency.

A shift in the focus of banks is visible with banks paying greater attention to customer needs and service. However, banks are now facing a number of challenges such as technological change, stringent prudential norms, increasing competition, worrying level of nonperforming assets (NPAs), rising customer expectations, increasing pressure on profitability, rising operating expenditure and increased risk in their lending operations. The spate of NPAs in the public sector banks has forced the government of India to recapitalize these banks early and often. The reforms in banking sector have also brought margins under pressure. The Reserve Bank of India's (RBI) efforts to adopt international banking norms such as *Basel III* norms is forcing banks to adopt measures to control and maintain margins.

In a recent Report on the Trend and Progress of Banking in India (2017) the RBI has observed that asset quality of the Indian banking sector is extremely poor. It is found that banks have faced a significant erosion in margins, with public sector banks suffering more than their private sector counterparts. Among the key challenges in going forward the RBI lists resolution of impaired assets and strengthening bank balance sheets, moving towards activity based rather than entity based regulation with the gradual implementation of *Basel III* norms, promoting technology based financial services and managing cyber security risks. Thus, banks will potentially be faced with reworking their business models to satisfy customer needs, clean up their balance sheets, improve corporate governance and leverage technology to meet security threats.

In the recent years the Reserve Bank of India (RBI) has embarked on a cycle of monetary easing following the sluggish growth trends in the Indian economy. This has caused banking stocks in India to rally sharply. However, all is not well as it seems in the banking sector. Recent quarterly reports of most banks suggest rising levels of nonperforming assets (NPAs) and deteriorating asset quality. Efforts to adopt international banking norms such as *Basel III* have further forced banks to take notice of capital adequacy requirements. Given that the banking sector is the lifeblood of the Indian economy, it is of paramount interest to understand what drives bank profitability. Under these circumstances it would be useful to examine the factors determining profitability of commercial banks in India.

1.2 Statement of the Problem

The banking industry in India is diverse in nature. There are more than sixty listed commercial banks in India. These include banks in the public and private sector and the banks are of varying size and profitability levels. As noted early, the Indian banking system is faced with severe asset quality issues. The banking system has been flooded with non-performing assets which have significantly eroded the bank margins. Recent adverse developments in the banking sector such as lending scams and questionable advances to troubled segments of the economy have dominated the financial press. While this being so, this research is aimed at examining the contributing factors of profitability in banks.

Key measures of bank profitability include the return of assets, return on equity and net interest margin. There are several possible drivers of bank profitability. These include asset quality, capital adequacy, liquidity, productivity and income. While several studies till date (**Chirwa, (2003)**; **Sufian and Habibullah, (2010)**; **Dietrich and Wanzenried, (2011)**; **Zarrouk et al., (2016)**) have looked at key determinants of bank profitability, very few studies have compared the effect of key determinants for a larger cross section of banks that represent the banking sector in India as a whole.

Hence an attempt has been made in this study to know the key drivers of profitability of the banking sector. The study also looks at the similarities or the differences of the influence of selected determinants on profitability measures across the sample of banks selected for research. This study also compares the key drivers of bank profitability for public and private sector banks and an attempt is made to develop models to forecast bank profitability from key determinants.

1.3 Research Questions

This study seeks to understand the impact of a series of key internal determinants of the profitability of listed commercial banks in India. Following are the research questions raised in this regard:

1) Are there differences in key performance measures of private and public sector banks?
2) Does the size of the bank affect bank profitability?
3) Does the bank's lending activity and income generation capability affect its profitability?
4) Does the productivity of the bank impact its profitability?
5) Does the bank's asset quality and capital adequacy affect its profitability?
6) Can bank profitability be forecasted from determinants?

1.4 Objectives of the Study

Taking into consideration the research questions raised, this research study has set the following objectives for examination:

1) To examine the differences in the profitability of private and public sector commercial banks in India.
2) To determine if bank size, lending and income measures impact bank profitability.
3) To determine the impact of productivity measures on the profitability of banks.
4) To find out the effect of capital adequacy and asset quality on the profitability of commercial banks.
5) To develop forecasting models based on key determinants identified by the study, to predict bank profitability.

1.5 Research Methodology

This study used historical data of select commercial banks to study the relationship between key determinants of profitability and important profitability measures. The sample consists of 24 Public sector banks and 16 private sector banks that have been listed for at least a 5 year period between the financial years ending March 2006 and March 2015. The following variables have been considered for the study:

Independent Variables:

Key bank metric - Bank size (S) as measured by market capitalization.

Key lending measure - The deposit to credit ratio (DCR).

Income Measures - Interest income to average working funds (IIAWF) and Noninterest income/average working funds (NIIAWF) which is a measure of fee based income.

Productivity measure - Business per employee (BPE).

Measure of Capital Adequacy - The capital adequacy ratio (CAR).

Measure of Asset Quality – The percentage net non-performing assets (NNPA).

Dependent Variables:

Bank Profitability as measured by the **Return on Assets (ROA)** and the **Return on Equity (ROE).**

The study was conducted with annual data for the ten year period spanning from the financial years 2006 to 2015. Data from 2016 and 2017 was used for forecasting purposes from models developed in the study. Historical data on all of the above were obtained from the *Capitaline* financial database and the Reserve Bank of India data base on the Indian economy. The relationship between the variables was analyzed with the SPSS 18.0 package. Q-Q plots were used to ascertain normality of the data. Descriptive statistics that includes mean, standard deviation and the co-efficient of variation were used to compare key performance measures of public and private banks.

Scatter plots and correlation analysis were used to study the relationship between the respective variables. F-values from ANOVA analysis were used to assess the statistical significance of the correlations observed at 95% confidence intervals. Then Uni-variate and multiple regression analysis were used to study the impact of all the independent variables taken individually and together on the profitability as measured by ROA and ROE of the respective banks.

The influencing determinants were used to construct multi-variate models which were then used to forecast ROA and ROE for the years ending March 2016 and March 2017. Variance Inflation Factor (VIF) was used to detect multi-collinearity. Durbin Watson coefficient was used to detect auto correlation in the data. The adjusted R^2 was used to determine the influencing variables.

The Breusch Pagan test was used to detect heteroskedasticity in the data. Given the presence of heteroskedasticity a robust estimation was performed using the quantile regression technique to estimate model parameters. The Akaike Criterion (AIC) was used to select the best model. The root mean squared error and mean absolute error were used to validate forecast accuracy. Further details on the research methodology are discussed in detail in Chapter 4.

1.6 Scope of the Study

This study had used historical data of select commercial banks to compare the relationship between key determinants of profitability and important profitability measures. The sample consists of 24 Public sector banks and 16 private sector banks that have been listed for at least a 5 year period between the financial years ending March 2006 and March 2015. Models developed were used to forecast profitability for the financial years ending March 2016 and March 2017.

1.7 Significance of the Study

The study could provide several key stake holders of banks valuable information on what drives profitability of commercial banks. It seeks to add to the existing body of literature on the impact of key determinants of profitability on bank profitability. A sound methodical approach is presented to examine the role of key determinants of profitability on two key profitability measures.

1.8 Limitations of the Study

The study only considered the impact of a select group of internal determinants on profitability of listed commercial banks in India. Only listed public sector and private sector banks that have been listed for a period of at least 5 years are considered for the study. Foreign banks listed in India are not considered in the study.

External determinants like macroeconomic factors and exchange rates are not considered. Additionally qualitative factors such as customer preferences and customer service are not considered. The impact of technology as a determinant is also not considered. In addition, the study also assumed variables vary linearly with each other which may not be the case, always.

1.9 Chapter Scheme

The first chapter introduces the study, its key objectives and the research problem. The second chapter provides an overview of the banking sector in India. The third chapter undertakes a review of literature in the field of research relevant to the study. The fourth chapter summarizes the research methodology adopted in the study. The fifth chapter presents the analysis of data and the results using relevant statistical tests. In the final chapter the findings and conclusion of the study are presented.

References

1) Chirwa, E. W. (2003). Determinants of commercial banks' profitability in Malawi: a cointegration approach. Applied Financial Economics, 13(8), 565–571.
2) Dietrich, A., & Wanzenried, G. (2011). Determinants of bank profitability before and during the crisis: Evidence from Switzerland. Journal of International Financial Markets, Institutions and Money, 21(3), 307–327.
3) Sufian, F., & Habibullah, M. S. (2010). Bank-specific, Industry-specific and Macroeconomic Determinants of Bank Efficiency: Empirical Evidence from the Thai Banking Sector. Margin: The Journal of Applied Economic Research (Vol. 4, pp. 427–461).
4) Zarrouk, H., Jedidia, K. Ben, & Moualhi, M. (2016). Is Islamic bank profitability driven by same forces as conventional banks? International Journal of Islamic and Middle Eastern Finance and Management, 9(1), 46–66.
5) Trend and Progress of Banking in India. (2017). Retrieved from https://www.rbi.org.in/scripts/AnnualPublications.aspx?head=Trend%20and%20Progress%20of%20Banking%20in%20India, Accessed, 14 Feb. 2018.

CHAPTER 2

BANKING SECTOR IN INDIA – A REVIEW

CHAPTER II

BANKING SECTOR IN INDIA – A REVIEW

Taking cues from RBI reports and other publications the overall banking landscape in India is summed up in this chapter. An elaborate discussion of the nature and functions of the Indian banking system is presented. The chapter is organized into 13 sub sections. The first two sub sections look at the emergence of banking across the globe and in India. The third and fourth sub sections look at the types of banks and their functions.

The next two sub sections look at key bank performance measures and a rating system for banks. Subsections seven and eight look at key risks encountered by banks and regulatory requirements. The emerging trends in Indian banking are discussed in sub section nine. Profitability measures and determinants of profitability are presented in the next two sub sections. The current banking scenario in India is reviewed in sub section twelve and the last subsection contains the operational definitions.

2.1 Origin of Banking

The word bank has French, Italian and German roots. The French word "Banqui" and the Italian word "Banca" refer to a bank as a bench. This reference to banks originated from money changers who engaged in transactions across benches. These money changers mainly dealt with different currencies and helped exchange one currency for another. Secondly the word bank could have also emerged from the German word "banck". The word banck was used to represent a joint stock company.

Banking traditions are deep rooted in history. The Bible has documented evidence of the activities of money changers during the times of Jesus Christ. In ancient Greece as early as 2000 B.C. the famous temples of Ephesus, Delphi and Olympia engaged in borrowing and lending serving as depositories and also facilitating lending as the need arose. The priests of these temples acted as custodians and helped facilitate depositing and lending of peoples funds. Credit transactions via transfer orders were also thought to have taken place initially in ancient Assyria, Phoenicia and Egypt and later on in Greece and Rome. In India, money lending and borrowing activities were found to have occurred in the ancient Vedic period (Hoggson, (1926)).

Public banking started in earnest around the middle of the twelfth century in Italy. The Bank of Venice, founded in 1157, was thought to be the first public banking institution. Almost three centuries following the establishment of the Bank of Venice, the Bank of Barcelona and the Bank of Genoa were founded in 1401 and 1407 respectively. The prestigious Bank of Amsterdam was established in Holland in 1609.

Modern banking commenced with the establishment of the Bank of Amsterdam. In the year 1694 the Bank of England was established. The Bank of England's establishment kick started a revolution in banking. Joint stock companies entered the banking space in the eighteenth century following the implementation of The Banking Act of 1833. This led to the development of commercial banking system across several countries and continents across the globe (Hoggson, (1926)).

2.2 Banking in India

Banking in India can be classified into two distinct phases, the pre and post-independence phases. The pre-independence phase lasted from 1786 to 1947 and the post-independence phase lasted from 1947 to the present time.

2.2.1 The Pre-Independence Phase

The establishment of the General Bank of India in the year 1786 marked the introduction of a structured banking system in India. It was setup as a joint stock company. Later the Bank of Hindustan and Bengal Bank came into existence. The East India Company established three banks. These were the Bank of Bengal in the year 1809, the

Bank of Bombay in 1840 and Bank of Madras in 1843. These three Banks were amalgamated in year 1920 to form the new Imperial Bank of India.

Between 1865 and 1906 three more banks came into existence. These were Allahabad Bank, Punjab National Bank and the Bank of India. The Bank of Baroda, Canara Bank, The Central Bank of India, Indian Bank and Bank of Mysore came into existence between 1906 and 1913. The Reserve Bank of India (RBI) was constituted as the shareholder's bank in 1935 and was now the Central Bank of the Country ("The Advent of Modern Banking in India").

2.2.2 The Post-Independence Phase

Since banking services were inaccessible to most of the Indian public the government of India began nationalization of the banking sector. After independence, the Reserve Bank of India Bill was introduced in the parliament to make it a public bank. Since 1st January 1949, the RBI has been operating as a state owned and operated Central Bank. It regulates the Indian banking industry. The Imperial Bank was nationalized and was renamed as the State Bank of India with the passing of the State Bank of India Act of 1955.

In 1969 the government of India nationalized fourteen banks whose deposit base exceeded rupees fifty crores. These were Allahabad Bank, Punjab National Bank, the Bank of India, the Bank of Baroda, Canara Bank, the Central Bank of India, Indian Bank, the Bank of Maharashtra, Dena Bank, Indian Overseas Bank, Syndicate Bank, United Bank and UCO Bank.

Even after the nationalization of these banks people in rural areas still did not have access to proper banking services. To address these issues the Narasimham Committee was set up and as per its recommendations in 1974, Regional Rural Banks (RRB's) were set up in October 1975 to increase the flow of credit to rural areas. In 1980 six more banks were nationalized. These were Andhra Bank, Vijaya Bank, Corporation Bank, The New Bank of India, Oriental Bank of Commerce and Punjab and Sindh Bank.

In 1990 as India embarked on economic reforms and opened up its economy the Narasimham Committee recommended a series of banking reforms intended to make the financial system stable and banks more competitive. These included stopping further bank nationalizations, enabling foreign banks to open subsidiaries in India, having a uniform regulatory process for both private and public banks, encouraging banks to take more risk and venture into higher growth areas such as underwriting, merchant banking and retail banking, encouraging joint ventures between foreign and Indian banks to offer value based financial services and allowing entry of more private players into the Indian banking space.

Based on the above recommendations several foreign banks like Citibank, Standard Charter Bank, Deutsche Bank etc. have entered the Indian banking space. These banks have partnered with several Indian banks to offer an array of financial services. Several private players like ICICI bank, HDFC bank, Axis Bank, Kotak Bank, Yes bank and more recently Bandhan bank and IDFC bank have emerged after having been granted licenses to enter the banking space in India. The detailed summary of events in the post-independence phase from 1967 to 1985 is shown below ("Reserve Bank of India - Chronology of Events"):

Table 2.1 Chronology of Events in the Banking Sector in India in the Post-Independence Phase

Date	Event
December-67	Introduction of Social Controls over banks to align the banking system to the requirements of economic policy.
22-December-67	National Credit Council was set up to assist the RBI and the government in allocating credit.
1-April-68	Quarternary alloy Rupee coins were demonetised.
1-September-68	Gold (Control) Act was passed to control the purchase and sale of gold

1968	Export credit scheme, and pre-shipment Credit scheme were introduced to promote exports.
29-January-69	The banking commission was set up by the government of India to monitor banking costs, legislations affecting banking, indigenous banking, bank procedures and non-banking financial intermediaries.
1-February-69	Gold Holdings of RBI were revalued at the current official IMF rate following the over 35% devaluation of the Rupee.
19-July-69	14 major Indian Scheduled Commercial Banks with deposits of over Rs. 50 crores were nationalized.
December-69	Lead bank scheme was introduced to address credit gaps in the economy.
1-January-70	Special Drawing Rights (SDR) were created by the IMF to enhance international liquidity.
January-70	RBI set for the first time the minimum interest rate to be charged by banks on advances against sensitive commodities.
February-70	The Agricultural Credit Board was set up to formulate and review policies in the sphere of rural credit.
Between February & August 1970	Inflationary concerns led to the RBI increasing the bank rate and raising the SLR from 25 to 28%.
1-November-70	New bills rediscounting scheme was introduced to improve the money market and enable the RBI to exercise more effective control over the money market.
14-January-71	Credit Guarantee Corporation of India Ltd. Was established to facilitate bank lending to the priority sectors.
12-April-71	Concerns on industrial sickness led to the establishment of the Industrial Reconstruction Corporation of India Ltd.

Date	Event
1-July-71	Deposit Insurance cover was extended to cooperative banks.
15-August-71	Convertibility of the USD was suspended. This brought to an end the system of fixed exchange rates specified in the Bretton Woods System and the world shifted to a floating exchange rate regime.
October-71	State Level Bankers' Committees were set up to consider problems requiring inter-bank coordination.
25-March-72	Differential interest rate scheme was introduced which provided concessional interest rates on advances made by public sector banks to selected low income groups.
3-November-72	Special payment arrangements were made with the COMECON group of countries where payments were settled in rupees through bilateral trade.
1973	The oil shock occurred when oil prices quadrupled. This led to double digit inflation as well as a global recession.
1973	As a response the RBI deployed a series of restricted measures to moderate the expansion of bank credit.
1973	Call money rates rose to an all-time high of 30% prompting the Indian Banks' Association to intervene and fix a ceiling of 15%.
1-September-73	Miscellaneous Non-Banking Companies Direction, 1973 sought to regulate the acceptance of deposits by companies conducting prize chits, lucky draws savings schemes, etc.
8-September-73	Quantitative credit ceiling on non-food bank credit was prescribed for the first time.
November-73	Restrictions on SBI and its subsidiaries were removed to bring them on par with other commercial banks.
1-January-74	The Foreign Exchange Regulation Act, 1973 came into force and was entrusted to the RBI.

9-December-74	Asian Clearing Union (ACU) was established to facilitate payments for current international transactions on a multilateral basis.
13-December-74	Reserve Bank of India (Amendment) Act, 1974 widened the powers of the RBI.
9-August-75	Tandon Committee Report emphasized the need to correlate bank credit to production plans and resources of borrowers.
	The new norms formed the basis of bank lending for working capital requirements.
25-September-75	Exchange rate of the Rupee was linked to movements in a basket of selected foreign currencies.
26-September-75	Regional Rural Banks were set up to increase rural credit.
1-November-75	Foreign Currency (Non Resident) Account Scheme was introduced in USD and GBP to encourage private remittances from abroad.
1975	The 20 point economic programme was introduced.
1-February-76	Duty draw back credit scheme was introduced to promote exports.
1976	Village Adoption Scheme for banks was introduced.
April-77	Concepts of M1, M2, M3 money supply were introduced
2-May-77	M. Narasimham appointed Governor up to November 30 who later pioneered the Narasimham committee reforms.
1977	Integrated Rural Development Programme (IRDP) was initiated as a poverty alleviation measure.

16-January-78	Notes of Rs. 1,000/-, Rs. 5,000/- and Rs. 10,000/- denominations were demonetised to curb illicit financial transactions.
3-May-78	RBI started gold auctions on behalf of the Government of India.
3-June-78	RBI Act was amended to enable the more effective utilization of foreign exchange reserves.
12-December-78	Prize, chit and money circulation schemes were banned with effect 12 December, 1978.
1978	Annual appraisal of banks, in the form of a management audit was introduced.
30-March-79	Penalty for non-compliance of CRR & SLR was introduced to help the RBI implement monetary policy measures more effectively.
1979	Rural Planning and Credit Cell set up in the RBI to promote credit in rural areas.
August-79	Credit information review was published every month to disseminate in simple language the credit and banking policy decisions of the Reserve Bank.
March-80	Banks were required to provide financial support to the implementation of the 20 point programme to improve weaker segments of society.
15-April-80	Six private sector banks were nationalized
December-80	Recommendations of the Chore Committee related to the cash credit system were adopted. Emphasis was on increasing contribution towards working capital requirements by borrowers out of internal resources.
15-January-81	The government of India announced a special bearer bond to mop up unaccounted money.

April-81	Major organizational internal restructuring in the RBI with the creation of new departments.
1981	Inflationary pressures and adverse movement in foreign trade followed the hike in oil prices. Bank rate was raised to 10%, CRR was raised to 7.5%, and SLR to 35% by the RBI.
1-January-82	Export Import Bank of India established with the objective of providing financial and allied services to exporters and importers.
1-January-82	New 20 point programme was announced.
12-July-82	National Bank for Agriculture and Rural Development (NABARD) was established for the promotion of agriculture, small scale industries, cottage industries, village industries, handicrafts, and other rural industries.
November-83	National Clearing Cell (NCC) set up by the RBI to introduce mechanized cheque processing and nationwide cheque clearing.
12-January-84	Banking Laws (Amendment) Act, 1983 widened the activities that banks could undertake (such as leasing), provided nomination facilities to account holders, strengthened the powers of the RBI, streamlined returns and prohibited unincorporated bodies from accepting deposits from the public.
1-February-84	Urban Banks Department was formed to supervise the affairs of Urban Cooperative Banks.

Source RBI

2.3 Classification of Banks

The banking structure in India is described below and shows the different types of banks that are part of India's banking system:

Figure 2.1: Classification of Banks

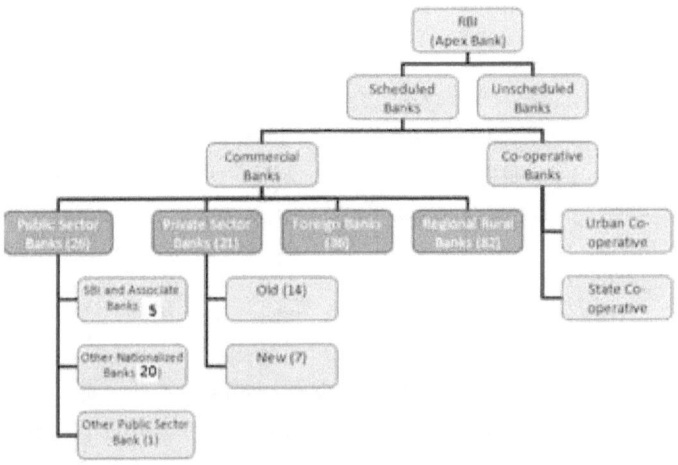

Source: Jagranjosh.com

2.3.1 The Reserve Bank of India

The RBI is India's apex bank and the absolute banking regulatory authority in India. The RBI was established on April 1935 as the central bank of India. It was nationalized in January 1949. The RBI performs some key functions such as being the government's banker, the note issuing authority of India, the banker's bank, the regulator of money and credit and exercising supervisory authority over the entire banking system. Under this authority the RBI regulates affairs of all players in the Indian financial system under the RBI Act of 1934 and the Banking Regulation Act of 1949.

2.3.2 Scheduled Banks

Scheduled banks are those that are included and regulated under the second schedule of the RBI act of 1934. These banks are required to have a minimum paid up capital and reserve of Rupees twenty-five lakhs. Most commercial banks that include public sector, private sector, co-operative and foreign banks operating in India would fall under this category. These banks can borrow money from the RBI for their regular banking activities and have to maintain their Cash Reserve Ratio (CRR) requirements with the RBI.

2.3.3 Unscheduled Banks

Unscheduled or non-scheduled banks are those that are not included and regulated under the second schedule of the RBI act of 1934. These banks cannot borrow money from the RBI for their regular banking activities. They have to maintain their Cash Reserve Ratio (CRR) requirements but not with the RBI.

2.3.4 Commercial Banks

These are banks which provide services to businesses, organizations and individuals. The main function of commercial banks is to accept deposits and advance loans. Deposits can be demand deposits, fixed deposits and savings deposits. Loans may be either cash credit, demand loans or short term loans. The commercial banks in India are further classified as public sector, private sector, region rural and foreign banks.

2.3.4.1 Public Sector Banks

Public sector banks are majority owned by the government implying that the government owns at least a 51% stake in them. This group of banks includes all nationalized banks. State Bank of India is India's largest public sector bank. There are over twenty public sector banks in India. All listed public sector banks are shown in the table below. State Bank of India is the largest public sector bank in India having the largest market capitalization and asset base. It is also the most profitable public sector bank.

Table 2.2 Public Sector Banks in India

Bank	Market Capitalization (Rs. Crores)	Net Interest Income (Rs. Crores)	Net Profit (Rs. Crores)	Total Assets (Rs. Crores)
State Bank of India	213163.77	175518.24	10484.1	2705966.3
Bank of Baroda	33518.69	42199.93	1383.13	694875.41
Punjab National Bank	20635.28	47995.76	-12282.82	720330.55

IDBI Bank	18641.95	27791.37	-5158.14	361767.9
Central Bank	17633.28	24035.51	-5104.91	333401.95
Canara Bank	17282.58	41252.09	-4222.24	583519.45
Bank of India	16288.13	39290.87	-1558.34	626309.27
Indian Bank	14435.17	17113.65	1258.99	218233.15
Union Bank	9728.37	32748	-5247.37	452704.45
Indian Overseas Bank	7825.23	19718.61	-3416.74	247167.49
Vijaya Bank	7642.31	12589.84	727.02	154881.58
Syndicate Bank	6136.79	21775.95	-3222.84	299073.34
State Bank of Bikaner	5402.95	9592.47	850.6	110336.27
Oriental Bank	4771.07	17398.89	-5871.74	253064.72
State Bank of Travancore	4328.47	9608.88	337.73	114506.78
UCO Bank	4189.31	14020.13	-4436.37	231339.7
Corporation Bank	4188.85	19471.47	561.21	247891.04
Andhra Bank	4117.99	18027.42	174.34	222126.12
Dena Bank	3693.54	8932.23	-1923.15	129623.55
Bank of Maharashtra	3416.97	11096.42	-1145.65	159323.98
United Bank	3405	9427.91	219.51	141053.12
Allahabad Bank	3186.27	16358.49	-4674.37	237037.89
State Bank of Mysore	2909.85	7127.78	357.85	82975
Punjab & Sind Bank	1807.72	7948.75	-743.8	96643.44

Source: Moneycontrol.com as on 20/5/2019

2.3.4.2 Private Sector Banks

Private sector banks are banks where a major equity stake is held by private shareholders. The private banking sector has emerged post the liberalization phase in India in 1993. Examples of these banks are HDFC Bank, Kotak Bank, Axis Bank etc. There are over fifteen private sector banks in India. All listed private sector banks are shown in the table below. HDFC bank is the largest private sector bank in India having the largest market capitalization and asset base. It is also the most profitable private sector bank.

Table 2.3 Private Sector Banks in India

Bank	Market Capitalization (Rs. Crores)	Net Interest Income (Rs. Crores)	Net Profit (Rs. Crores)	Total Assets (Rs. Crores)
HDFC Bank	522550.46	80241.35	17486.75	863840.2
Kotak Mahindra	246683.5	19748.49	4084.3	214589.96
ICICI Bank	183933.34	54965.89	6777.42	771791.46
Axis Bank	136829.08	45780.31	275.68	601467.66
IndusInd Bank	115848.56	17280.75	3605.99	178648.43
Yes Bank	79623.33	20267.42	4224.56	312445.6
Bandhan Bank	57200.96	4802.3	1345.56	30236
RBL Bank	21340.09	4507.57	635.09	48674.78
ING Vysya Bank	19719.13	5205.22	657.85	60413.23
Federal Bank	16275.73	9752.86	878.85	114976.93
IDFC Bank	13956.84	8930	859.3	112159.66
City Union Bank	12560.06	3173.79	502.77	35270.78
Karur Vysya Bank	7226.43	5622.35	605.98	61807.61
DCB Bank	5584.72	2412.99	245.34	30222.09
South India Bank	4632.32	6192.81	334.89	74312.15
Karnataka Bank	3409.42	5423.75	325.61	64126.55
Jamu and Kashmir Bank	2865.04	6685.8	-1632.29	82018.66
Lakshmi Vilas Bank	2375.62	2846.66	256.07	35244.71
Dhanlaxmi Bank	469.34	1089.05	12.38	12333.12

Source: Moneycontrol.com as on 20/5/2019

2.3.4.3 Foreign Banks

These banks are headquartered overseas but operate subsidiaries in India. There are over thirty five foreign banks in India. Examples of foreign banks include HSBC, Citibank, Standard Chartered Bank etc.

2.3.4.4 Regional Rural Banks

As per the recommendation of the Narasimham Committee regional rural banks (RRB's) were set up in 1975 to increase the flow of credit to agriculture and other rural segments. Regional rural banks are jointly owned by the government of India, the concerned state government and sponsor banks in the ratio 50:15:35 respectively. Prathama bank is an example of one such RRB in rural Uttar Pradesh.

2.3.5 Co-operative Banks

A co-operative bank is owned by its members who are at the same time its owners and customers. These banks are created my members of a local community to further common grounds of interest. They provide members with a wide range of banking and financial services such as bank accounts, loans and deposits. Co-operative banks operate on the "no-profit no-loss" principle. They are further classified into urban and state co-operative banks.

2.4 Function of Banks

There are some key functions that are performed by banks (Suresh & Paul, 2014). These are shown in figure 1.7. These include:

(I) Primary Functions that include Accepting Deposits and Granting Loans and

(II) Secondary Functions that include Agency Functions and General Utility Functions.

Figure 2.2 Function of Banks

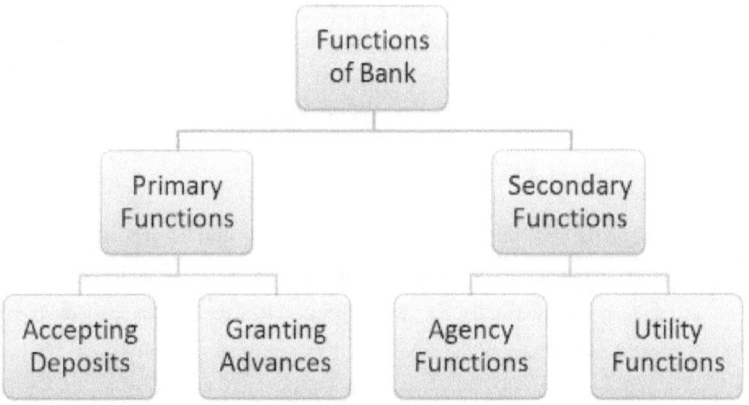

2.4.1 Primary Functions

The primary functions of modern banks include accepting deposits and advancing loans (Suresh & Paul, 2014):

2.4.1.1 Accepting Deposits

One of the most important functions of a commercial bank is to accept deposits from the public. Banks require large sums of money for their lending activities. Therefore, banks accept deposits from individuals or companies and pay interest on deposited funds. Individuals and companies deposit their surplus funds with banks for both safe keeping and earning interest. Banks pay the appropriate interest on the deposits collected. The bank not only guarantees the deposit but also agrees to meet the demands of the depositors arising from any withdrawals required. Banks generally provide the following deposit accounts:

2.4.1.1.1 Fixed Deposit Account

This is also referred to as a term deposit or time deposit account. Money in this account is accepted for a fixed period, usually between one and ten years. The money so deposited cannot be withdrawn before the maturity period. The rate of interest on this account is usually higher than that on other accounts and varies according to the time period of the deposit. It matures at the end of the fixed period. If a depositor withdraws this amount before the maturity period, he incurs an interest penalty. Thus, banks have these funds at their disposal for a certain fixed period.

2.4.1.1.2 Current Account

This is also known as a demand deposit or current deposit account. Here the depositor can withdraw the money from this account as and when he requires it. Usually, the bank pays no interest on this account because it has to keep the cash ready at all times to meet the requirement of the depositors. This account is generally opened by companies, institutions or even the government, who engage in cash transactions several times in a day. In the case of a current account, the bank has to pay either the depositor himself or a third party whom the depositor authorizes by issuing cheques. Overdraft facilities are usually made available on current accounts.

2.4.1.1.3 Savings Account

This type of account is generally opened by individuals. They deposit their savings in this account and earn interest on the amount deposited. Deposits in this account earn interest at nominal rates, as these can be redeemed by the depositor without notice. In practice, the bank imposes a limit on the number and amount of withdrawals that can be done during any given period. The depositors can also issue cheques against this account.

2.4.1.1.4 Other Accounts

Banks also provide other types of accounts as per the requirement of the customer. Some popular accounts offered by banks are Indefinite Period Deposit Accounts, Recurring Deposit Accounts, Daily Saving Deposit Accounts, Home Safe Accounts, Retirement Schemes, Monthly Income Schemes, Minor Saving Accounts, Farmers Deposit Account, Home Deposit Account and Accounts related to Insurance benefits.

2.4.1.2 Advancing Loans

A very important function of commercial bank is advancing loans to their customers. Given that banks receive deposits from their customers they are obligated to pay interest on the deposits received. Banks channel the available amount from deposits into loans and charge higher rates of interest on them. These loans are usually granted to traders, industrialists, farmers and self-employed individuals. Generally, banks sanction the following type of loans and advances.

2.4.1.2.1 Cash Credit

Banks advance loans against certain collateral. Collateral can be securities such as shares and debentures, goods and tangible assets. Cash credit may be granted also on the promissory notes of borrowers. Banks grant loans and deposit them in the borrowers account. The borrower can withdraw this amount at any time and interest is charged on the borrowed amount. The borrower cannot exceed the credit limit sanctioned to him. The collateral of the borrower in the form of goods (stock) is kept in a warehouse which remains in the possession of the bank till the borrowed amount is repaid.

2.4.1.2.2 Loans and Advances

The bank lends a specified sum of money to a person or a firm against some collateral. The loaned money is credited to the account of the borrower and the borrower can withdraw the amount according to his requirements. The borrower has to pay interest on the entire amount of the loan from the date of sanctioning of the loan to the date of repayment. If the borrower fails to repay the loan, the pledged collateral can be sold by the bank in the market to recover the loan sanctioned.

2.4.1.2.3 Overdraft

Commercial banks provide customers with an overdraft facility, where the customer can issue cheques up to a certain amount greater than the balance lying in his account. In the case of use of the overdraft, a customer pays interest on the amount by which his current account is overdrawn. He is not required to pay interest on the entire amount of the overdraft sanctioned to him by the bank. This facility is usually granted against some collateral for a short period.

2.4.1.2.4 Discounting of Bills of Exchange

Banks also discount bills of exchange for their customers. In case a holder of a bill needs money immediately, he can get his bills discounted by the bank. The bank charges a commission for discounting. When the bill matures, the bank can get the proceeds directly from the original issuer of the bill.

2.4.2 Secondary Functions:

The secondary functions of banks comprise of agency and general utility functions (Suresh & Paul, 2014):

2.4.2.1 Agency or Representative Functions

Banks perform several agency functions or services for their customers. For these services, the bank charges commissions from its customers. Some services are provided by the bank to its customers free of charge. The various agency services rendered by the bank are as follows:

2.4.2.1.1 Collection of Cheques, Bills of Exchange and other Credit Instruments

Banks collect payments on cheques, bills of exchange and other credit instruments on behalf of their customers from other banks and credit their accounts. Generally, this service is rendered free of charge but on some credit instruments, banks may charge a nominal fee.

2.4.2.1.2 Making Payment via Cheque, Bills of Exchange etc.

Commercial banks perform the function of making payments through cheques, bills of exchange etc. Banks pay insurance premiums, rent, subscriptions etc. on behalf of their customers. Banks also accept bills of exchange on behalf of their customers and make payments as and when due.

2.4.2.1.3 Collecting dividends, interest etc. on shares and debentures of the customers

Banks receive dividends and interest paid on shares and debentures of companies held by their customers on their behalf and credits them in their account.

2.4.2.1.4 Remittance Facilities

On request of their customers, banks help in transferring funds from one account to another through bank drafts, cheques, and electronic transfers. Banks charge fees for these services rendered.

2.4.2.1.5 Purchase and Sale of Securities

Banks help their customers purchase and sell shares and debentures in the market by providing their customers with dematerialization (DEMAT) accounts. This helps customers to transact securities securely in electronic form. They charge appropriate commissions for their services.

2.4.2.1.6 Trustee and Executor

Banks also perform the functions of trustees, executors, administrators and attorneys. As a trustee, banks oversee the assets of the customers. They also help in the administration of trusts set up by their customers. As an executor banks execute wills of the customers as per their request. As an attorney, banks signs transfer forms and documents on behalf of the customer.

2.4.2.1.7 Underwriting Function

Banks also perform the function of underwriting shares, debentures, bonds and other securities issued by public limited companies or the Government. By becoming the underwriter banks guarantee subscription to the issued securities. The underwriting function of banks creates public confidence in the new issue market for securities. Banks charge appropriate commissions for the underwriting services provided.

2.4.2.1.8 Other Agency Functions

Banks also act as agents, representatives or correspondents of their customers. The bank may obtain passports, tickets for travel etc. to satisfy its customer's requirements.

2.4.2.2 General Utility Functions

Banks also provide the following general utility services to its customers:

2.4.2.2.1 Facilities for Safe Custody of Valuable Goods

Banks make available locker facilities to their customers for keeping their valuables like share and debentures certificates, gold and silver jewelry, documents etc. Banks charge annual rent for the locker facilities provided.

2.4.2.2.2 Issue of Travelers Cheques

Banks may also issue travelers cheques or circular letters of credit for the benefit of their customers. Customers can use these while travelling abroad for their transaction requirements.

2.4.2.2.3 Providing Information to its Customers

Since banks work with several customers, they can pass on reliable information about the credit-worthiness of third parties to their customers. The banks information is often considered reliable by customers who could use it while transacting with third parties. This helps their customers manage their risk better.

2.4.2.2.4 Financial Advisor

As banks are fully acquainted with the economic developments in the nation, they are in a position to render useful advice to its customers on financial matters. This helps the customer in taking appropriate investment decisions.

2.4.2.2.5 Publication of Statistics

Large commercial banks publish statistics about money, banking, trade and commerce. This is useful to their customers and helps them in taking economic and business decisions.

2.4.2.2.6 Accepting Bills of Exchange:

Banks accept bills of exchange on behalf of their customers. This benefits the customers because they have a quick access to funds. This is possible because as and when the bank accepts the bill it becomes readily discountable in the money market.

2.4.2.2.7 Guarantor of Loans:

Commercial banks act as guarantors of loans granted by National and International Financial Institutions. This helps their customers to gain access to a wide range of loans easily.

2.4.2.2.8 Providing Consumer Loans:

Commercial banks grant consumer loans to their customers based on their personal credit worthiness that can be repaid in affordable installments.

2.4.2.2.9 Sale of Government Debt:

Commercial banks facilitate the selling of securities issued by the Government as agents of the RBI. This includes Treasury Bills and Bonds issued by the government.

2.4.2.2.10 Facilitator of Foreign Exchange:

Commercial banks also make foreign exchange available to their customers as and when required.

2.4.2.3 Other Functions:

Other than the above mentioned functions banks perform a few other important functions like making arrangements for foreign trade and creation of credit:

2.4.2.3.1 Making Arrangements for Foreign Trade:

Commercial banks have played an important role in the expansion of foreign trade. They make available short term credit to traders engaged in foreign trade through the acceptance of letters of credit and discounting of bills. These transactions were popular as early as the medieval period. Thus banks help in establishing important relationships between exporters and importers and help in facilitating international trade.

2.4.2.3.2 Credit Creation:

Commercial banks play an important role in creating credit in the economy. They facilitate this by granting loans and advances. When the bank grants loans to its customers, it generally does not lend out cash as an individual money-lender does, but opens an account in the borrowers name and credits the amount of the loan into his account. Thus, whenever a bank grants a loan, it creates a deposit or a liability against itself, which leads to a net increase in the money supply in the economy. In this way banks create credit in the economy.

2.5 Key Bank Performance Measures

There are several key ratios which measure bank performance in several key operational areas such as liquidity, income generation, cost efficiency, lending and profitability. Some of these ratios are discussed below:

2.5.1 The Credit Deposit Ratio

This ratio is a key lending measure. It indicates how much a bank lends out as a function of the deposits it has received. In other words it shows how much of the mobilized funds are being used for the bank's core lending activity. A higher ratio indicates the bank's dependence on deposits as a source for lending and vice-versa.

A very low ratio indicates banks are not making full use of the resources at their disposal. A very high ratio is considered a warning sign and may have direct implications in deteriorating asset quality. The table below shows this important metric for Indian public sector and Indian private sector and foreign banks over the last nine years:

Table 2.4 Credit Deposit Ratios of Indian Banks

Year	Credit Deposit Ratio (%)	
	Public Banks	Private and Foreign Banks
2009	75.94	77.85
2010	75.45	76.25
2011	76.73	77.57
2012	78.89	81.03
2013	80.12	82.76
2014	79.96	83.34
2015	79.06	84.06
2016	78	86.29
2017	75.35	85.82

Source: Capitaline Database

2.5.2 The Investment Deposit Ratio

This ratio is a key liquidity measure. It measures the percentage of investments made by a bank both short and long term as a function of its deposits. A higher ratio implies that the bank has adequate liquidity to make relevant investments and signifies better financial health. However if the ratio is too high it may imply that the bank may not be prudent with its investments which could result in deteriorating asset quality in the future. The table below shows this important metric for Indian public sector and Indian private sector and foreign banks over the last nine years:

Table 2.5 Investment Deposit Ratios of Indian Banks

Year	Investment Deposit Ratio (%)	
	Public Banks	Private and Foreign Banks
2009	32.22	45.08
2010	32.52	47.26
2011	31.63	47.4
2012	30.32	48.08
2013	30.26	49.74
2014	30.03	48.01
2015	29.22	43.31
2016	28.36	40.9
2017	30.41	38.48

Source: Capitaline Database

2.5.3 Other Income to Total Income Ratio

This ratio is a measure of income diversification. It looks at the proportion of income generated from income other than interest income. Other income consists of primarily fees, brokerage commissions and income from treasury operations. This serves to provide diversification to the banks traditional interest income stream. A higher ratio indicates better income diversification. The table below shows this important metric for Indian public sector and Indian private sector and foreign banks over the last nine years:

Table 2.6 Other Income to Total Income Ratios of Indian Banks

Year	Other Income to Total Income Ratio (%)	
	Public Banks	Private and Foreign Banks
2009	13.29	22.79
2010	13.44	21.44
2011	11.29	19.97
2012	9.21	17.21
2013	9.07	16.34
2014	9.24	17.15
2015	9.81	17.71
2016	10.4	17
2017	13.89	19.49

Source: Capitaline Database

2.5.4 Operating Expenses to Total Income Ratio

This ratio is a measure of cost efficiency of a bank. It looks at operating expenses of a bank as a function of its total income generated. It indicates how well a bank is controlling its operating expenses relative to the income it generates. Lower the ratio better is the cost efficiency. The table below shows this important metric for Indian public sector and Indian private sector and foreign banks over the last nine years:

Table 2.7 Operating Expenses to Total Income Ratios of Indian Banks

Year	Operating Expenses to Total Income Ratio (%)	
	Public Banks	Private and Foreign Banks
2009	17.36	23.4
2010	18.23	24.34
2011	19.72	25.57
2012	16.57	23
2013	16.35	21.98
2014	17.24	21.77
2015	17.25	21.79
2016	18.21	21.82
2017	18.96	22.58

Source: Capitaline Database

2.5.5 Interest Income to Total Funds Ratio

This ratio is a measure of a bank's core income generation activity. Banks predominantly generate income through interest on loans and advances. This ratio indicates the extent to which a bank generates income as a function of its available funds. A healthy interest income percentage is mandatory for banks. However if this ratio is too high, it could indicate the absence of diversification. Too low a ratio would imply that the banks operations are hindered and would serve as a warning sign. The table below shows this important metric for Indian public sector and Indian private sector and foreign banks over the last nine years:

Table 2.8 Interest Income to Total Funds Ratios of Indian Banks

Year	Interest Income to Total Funds Ratio (%)	
	Public Banks	Private and Foreign Banks
2009	8.04	8.37
2010	7.44	7.26
2011	7.5	7.27
2012	8.5	8.21

2013	8.49	8.56
2014	8.29	8.38
2015	8.1	8.23
2016	7.78	8.32
2017	6.94	7.85

Source: Capitaline Database

2.5.6 Interest Expended to Total Funds Ratio

This ratio is a measure of a bank's major expenditure. Banks predominantly incur expenditure on their interest expense due on deposits and their borrowings in the capital market. This ratio indicates the extent to which a bank incurs interest expenditure as a function of its available funds. The lower this ratio higher will be the bank's net interest margin. The table below shows this important metric for Indian public sector and Indian private sector and foreign banks over the last nine years:

Table 2.9 Interest Expended to Total Funds Ratios of Indian Banks

Year	Interest Expended to Total Funds Ratio (%)	
	Public Banks	Private and Foreign Banks
2009	5.67	5.06
2010	5.14	4.04
2011	4.74	3.96
2012	5.76	4.92
2013	5.94	5.2
2014	5.84	5.04
2015	5.76	4.89
2016	5.55	4.87
2017	4.9	4.49

Source: Capitaline Database

2.5.7 Net Profit to Total Funds Ratio

This ratio is a measure of a bank's profitability. This ratio indicates the extent to which a bank is profitable as a function of its available funds. Higher the ratio more profitable is the bank. Banks tend to maximize their net interest margins to achieve higher profitability. The table below shows this important metric for Indian public sector and Indian private sector and foreign banks over the last nine years:

Table 2.10 Net Profit to Total Funds Ratios of Indian Banks

Net Profit to Total Funds Ratio (%)	
Public Banks	Private and Foreign Banks
1.03	1.34
0.97	1.15
0.93	1.45
0.89	1.52
0.79	1.62
0.52	1.52
0.47	1.6
-0.16	1.43
0.02	1.37

Source: Capitaline Database

2.6 Rating Frame Work for Banks

Globally Banks are rated and compared through the CAMEL framework. Regulators use these ratings to monitor the performance of banks. Autonomy is often granted to banks which exceed key performance metrics as laid out in the CAMEL framework which is described below (Suresh & Paul, 2014):

2.6.1 CAMEL Rating

The CAMEL rating is a framework that rates banks based on five key performance areas. These are capital adequacy (C), asset quality (A), managerial efficiency (M), earnings quality (E) and liquidity (L). Each of these parameters is assessed on a scale of 1 to 10 that include a number of sub parameters with individual weightage. Finally an overall rating is given for each bank that ranges from A to E. These are as follows:

A – Sound in every aspect.

B – Sound but having moderate weaknesses.

C – Weakness in financial, operational or compliance domains that are a cause for regulatory concern.

D – Serious finance, operational and managerial weaknesses that could impact future viability.

E – Critical financial weaknesses that could result in immediate failure.

2.6.1.1 Capital Adequacy (C)

Capital adequacy measures the extent to which a bank is capitalized. It indicates the level of capital, the quality of capital and the current financial condition of the bank. It also measures the ability of management to raise additional capital as and when required. The capital adequacy of a bank can be measured by the Capital Adequacy Ratio, the Debt to Equity Ratio, the Advances to Assets Ratio and the Government Securities to Total Investments ratio.

2.6.1.1.1 Capital Adequacy Ratio

The capital adequacy ratio is a measure of capital as a function of risk weighted assets at the bank. The capital required is a sum of Tier 1 and Tier 2 capital. Tier 1 capital is a capital buffer for short term losses while Tier 2 capital is a buffer required in the event of insolvency. The ratio indicates whether the bank is adequately capitalized to absorb operational losses. As per Basel III norms, the RBI requires Indian banks to have a capital adequacy ratio of at least 9 percent.

2.6.1.1.2 Debt to Equity Ratio

This ratio indicates the degree of leverage of a bank. It indicates how much of the bank's business is financed through debt and how much through equity. Too high a ratio would imply that the financial risk is high and must be taken as a warning sign.

2.6.1.1.3 Advances to Assets Ratio

This ratio measures the advances made by the bank as a function of its asset base. Banks tend to increase this ratio over time to increase net interest margins. However, too high a ratio suggests aggressiveness in lending, which could result in lower asset quality down the line.

2.6.1.1.4 Government Securities to Total Investments Ratio

This ratio measures the proportion of government securities as a function of total investments. Government securities tend to be the most liquid and risk free assets. An increasing trend in this ratio would suggest that the bank's capital adequacy is improving.

2.6.1.2 Asset Quality (A)

The asset quality of a bank directly refers to the quality of assets on the bank's balance sheet. It indicates the trend, the amount and the extent of nonperforming assets on the balance sheet. It also looks at the provisioning for loan losses. It also looks at the diversification and quality of the bank's loan portfolio and the internal controls adopted in monitoring it. Asset quality can be measured by the Net NPAs to Total Assets ratio, the Net NPAs to Net Advances ratio, the Percentage Change in NPAs and the Total Investments to Total Assets ratio.

2.6.1.2.1 Net NPAs to Total Assets Ratio

This ratio is a key measure of asset quality and looks at the proportion of net nonperforming assets as a function of the bank's total assets. Higher the ratio lower will be the asset quality. Banks need to monitor and control their non-performing assets to improve their asset quality.

2.6.1.2.2 Net NPAs to Net Advances Ratio

This ratio is a widely used measure of asset quality and looks at the proportion of net nonperforming assets as a function of the advances made by the bank. Higher the ratio lower will be the asset quality. Banks need to monitor their loans and reduce nonperforming assets to improve their asset quality.

2.6.1.2.3 Percentage Change in NPAs

This measure looks at the year on year percentage change in NPA levels. Increases in this metric would imply declining asset quality and vice versa. This metric helps to gage whether the asset quality of the bank is improving or declining over time.

2.6.1.2.4 Total Investments to Total Assets ratio

This ratio measures the investments made by a bank as a function of its asset base. The assets of a bank can be channeled into loans or investments. A higher ratio would indicate the preference of banks to invest in high quality assets and hence higher asset quality.

2.6.1.3 Management Efficiency (M)

Management efficiency looks at the ability of the management and the board of directors to improve performance and control risks at the bank. It looks at the quality of the supervisory framework adopted by the banks management to get the best out of its employees. It also looks at the effect of managerial policies in place in key areas such as succession planning and compensation. Management efficiency can be measured by four key ratios. These are the Total Advances to Total Deposits ratio, the Profit per Employee, the Business per Employee and the Return on Net Worth.

2.6.1.3.1 Total Advances to Total Deposits Ratio

This ratio is a key lending measure. It indicates how much a bank lends out as a function of the deposits it has received. In other words it shows how much of the mobilized funds are being used for the bank's core lending activity. A higher ratio indicates the bank's dependence on deposits as a source for lending and vice-versa. A very low ratio indicates banks are not making full use of the resources at their disposal. A very high ratio is considered a warning sign and may have direct implications in deteriorating asset quality.

2.6.1.3.2 Profit per Employee

The profit per employee is a productivity measure and measures the profit generated by each employee on an average. A rising trend in this ratio would imply that management is increasingly able to generate more profits from its employees which in turn is an indication of managerial efficiency.

2.6.1.3.3 Business per Employee

The business per employee is also a productivity measure and measures the business generated by each employee on an average. The primary business of a bank is obtaining deposits and sanctioning loans. A rising trend in this ratio would imply that management is able to generate more business from its employees which in turn is an indication of managerial efficiency.

2.6.1.3.4 Return on Net Worth

The return on net worth also referred to as the return on equity (ROE) is widely followed by investors. It shows how profitable a bank is relative to its equity base. The ROE of a bank indicates how well the banks management deploys share holder funds to generate profits. In other words the ROE of a bank gives you the returns for each dollar invested in it. Higher the ROE better the bank. Investors in banks tend to look for banks whose ROE shows an increasing trend over time.

2.6.1.4 Earnings Quality (E)

Earnings quality evaluates the trend, level and stability of a bank's earnings. It also looks at sources of the bank's earnings and quality of the underlying earnings. Earnings quality can be assessed by looking at the Operating Profit to Average Working Funds ratio, the Percentage Growth in Net Profit, Interest Income to Total Funds ratio and the Return on Assets.

2.6.1.4.1 Operating Profit to Average Working Funds Ratio

This ratio measures the ability of a bank to generate operating profits from its available funds. Thus the bank must optimize its lending and investing activities to maximize this ratio. Higher this ratio, more profitable is the banks key operational activities.

2.6.1.4.2 Percentage Growth in Net Profit

This measure indicates the trend in profit growth. It measures the annual change in net profit. A rising trend in this measure is a sign of improving net interest margins and increasing profitability.

2.6.1.4.3 Interest Income to Total Funds Ratio

This ratio is a measure of a bank's core income generation activity. Banks predominantly generate income through interest on loans and advances. This ratio indicates the extent to which a bank generates income as a function of its available funds. A healthy interest income percentage is mandatory for banks. However if this ratio is too high, it could indicate the absence of diversification in the banks income stream. Too low a ratio would imply that the banks operations are hindered and would serve as a warning sign.

2.6.1.4.4 Return on Assets

The Return on Assets (ROA) is the most widely used measure of bank profitability. It shows how profitable a bank is relative to its total asset base. The ROA of a bank indicates how efficient the bank's management is in deploying the bank's entire asset base to generate profits. The benchmark ROA is about 1 percent for banks globally. While banks must exceed their industry benchmark ROA, too high an ROA would imply that they are not reinvesting in assets for their future and must be taken as a warning sign.

2.6.1.5 Liquidity

Under the CAMEL framework liquidity implies that the bank has adequate liquid assets to cover present and future needs. Banks are required to have significant amounts of cash and cash equivalents, a stable source of deposits and access to money market instruments. Liquidity can be measured by the Liquid Assets to Demand Deposits ratio, the Liquid Assets to Total Assets ratio, the G-Secs to Total Assets ratio and the Approved Securities to Total Assets ratio.

2.6.1.5.1 Liquid Assets to Demand Deposits Ratio

This ratio measures liquid assets owned by the bank such as cash and cash equivalents as a function of its demand deposits. It indicates whether the bank has sufficient liquidity to meet the obligations from demand deposits. Higher this ratio, more liquid is the bank.

2.6.1.5.2 Liquid Assets to Total Assets Ratio

This ratio measures liquid assets owned by the bank such as cash and cash equivalents as a function of its asset base. It examines the proportion of assets held by the bank as liquid assets. Greater this ratio better is the liquidity position of the bank.

2.6.1.5.3 G-Secs to Total Assets Ratio

Government securities (G-Secs) such as T-bills and T-bonds that are issued by either the state or central government are the among most liquid and risk free assets available. This ratio looks at the fraction of total assets held in G-Secs by the bank. Higher this ratio better is the liquidity position of the bank.

2.6.1.5.4 Approved Securities to Total Assets Ratio

Approved securities are also highly liquid instruments of state government entities. This ratio looks at the fraction of total assets held in approved securities by the bank. Higher this ratio better is the liquidity position of the bank.

2.7 Risks Faced by Banks

There are several key risks encountered by banks. These include credit risk, market risk, operational risk, liquidity risk, business risk and systemic risk.

2.7.1 Credit Risk

Credit risk results from the possibility of default on loans by borrowers. This includes risk of not receiving payments as well as the risk posed by receiving delayed payments. Over the last five years most Indian banks have been saddled with a huge amount of nonperforming assets and this has caused a major source of credit risk for the Indian banking sector.

2.7.1.1 Nonperforming Assets

Nonperforming assets (NPA's) are loan accounts where either interest or installments of principal remain overdue for a period exceeding 90 days. Bills or other accounts that remain overdue for over 90 days are also classified as NPA's.

2.7.1.1.1 Classification of Nonperforming Assets

An asset is classified as a standard irregular asset if it remains outstanding as an NPA for over 90 days. An asset is treated as a sub-standard asset if it has remained as an NPA for a period not exceeding 12 months. If an asset has remained an NPA for a period greater than 12 months it is classified as a doubtful account. Assets that remain as NPA's for an exceedingly long period of time well in excess of 36 months are treated as loss assets and adequate provisioning must be made for them.

2.7.1.1.2 Gross and Net NPA

NPA's are measured on both gross and net basis. Gross NPA's are all assets of the bank that have been lent out which are unrecoverable. Net NPA's factor in provisioning and are calculated as Gross NPA's less provisions.

2.7.2 Market Risk

Banks actively engage in treasury operations and participate in financial markets. As such they are exposed to fluctuating equity, bond, commodity and foreign exchange prices that could significantly impact their trading operations. Thus banks must hedge against these risks using appropriate derivatives.

2.7.3 Operational Risk

Banks have numerous operational processes and procedures relating to several key functional areas such as loan sanctioning and monitoring, fund disbursement and payments processing. Controls are required in several of these key areas. If controls are bypassed as in the case of the recent PNB scam, significant operational losses can result.

2.7.4 Liquidity Risk

Liquidity risks occur when a bank is in danger of meeting its obligations to its depositors. Liquidity risk occurs primarily due to asset liability mismatches at the bank. Under the current scenario banks are able to manage liquidity pressures through the assistance of central banks like the RBI. The RBI lends to banks in the event of a shortage.

2.7.5 Business Risk

Business risk occurs when a bank's strategy fails. Banks typically have short and long term strategic goals. If any of these goals are called into question and the bank fails to accomplish its objectives, it could result in major losses for the bank. In the 2008 financial crisis banks in the U.S that issued subprime mortgages were the hardest hit following the collapse in real estate prices.

2.7.6 Systemic Risk

Systemic risk is risk that affects the entire financial system. Given banks are likely counter parties to each other in their lending and trading business the failure of one bank can send ripples through the system, increases counter party risk and cause other banks to fail as was observed in the subprime crisis of 2008. Given the nature of systemic risk and the fact that no bank is immune to it requires banks to have exceptionally good risk management strategies when such risks surface.

2.8 Banking Regulations and Regulatory Requirements

The RBI is the apex regulator of banks in India. It ensures that banks comply with all regulatory norms. Other than meeting CRR and SLR requirements banks must also comply with global regulatory norms such as the Basel III framework.

2.8.1 Cash Reserve Ratio (CRR) and Statutory Liquid Ratio (SLR)

Indian banks have to set aside a certain percentage of funds with the RBI to meet regulatory requirements. The main regulatory ratios are the Cash Reserve Ratio (CRR) and Statutory Liquid Ratio (SLR).

2.8.1.1 Cash Reserve Ratio (CRR)

Every commercial bank has to keep a certain minimum percentage as cash reserves with RBI referred to as the CRR. RBI uses this tool to increase or decrease the reserve requirement depending on whether it wants to decrease or increase the money supply. An increase in the CRR will make it mandatory on the part of the banks to hold a large proportion of their deposits in the form of deposits with the RBI. This will reduce the size of their deposits and they will lend less. This will in turn decrease the money supply. The current CRR is 4%.

2.8.1.2 Statutory Liquid Ratio (SLR)

The percentage of securities that commercial banks are required to maintain with the RBI in the form of gold or government approved securities before providing credit to the customers. Statutory Liquidity Ratio is determined and maintained by the Reserve Bank of India in order to control the expansion of bank credit. The current SLR is 19.5%.

2.8.2 Basel III Norms

Basel III norms are a series of global banking regulations intended to make banks more robust and financially sound. These norms were directed at helping banks set minimum capital requirements to overcome credit market and operational risks. These norms were also intended to help regulators come up with better measures to supervise the banking system by enabling them to understand the risk profile of banks and the risk management processes adopted by banks. Finally these measures were also intended to help market participants such as investors to understand a bank's risk position and compare it with its peers. The *Basel III* norms are summarized in the figure below:

Figure 2.3: *Basel III* **Norms**

Pillar 1 Minimum Capital Requirements	Pillar 2 Supervisory Review Process	Pillar 3 Market Discipline
Capital Requirements for ... **Credit Risk** - Standardized Approach - Foundation IRB Approach - Advanced IRB Approach **Market Risk** - Standardized Approach - Internal VaR Models **Operational Risk** - Basic Indicator Approach - (Alternative) Standardized Approach - Advanced Measurement Approaches	**Framework for Banks (ICAAP)** - Capital allocation, including - Risk management **Supervisory Framework** - Evaluation of internal systems of banks - Assessment of risk profile - Review of compliance with all regulations - Supervisory measures	**Disclosure Requirements for Banks** - Transparency for market participants concerning the bank's risk position (scope of application, risk management, detailed information on own funds, etc.) - Enhanced comparability among banks

FINANCIAL STABILITY

Source: Quora

The *Basel III* norms seek to address three key areas of importance for banks. These are capital requirements, leverage and liquidity.

2.8.2.1 Capital Requirements

Basel III norms require banks to account for more of the risk they take on their books. Thus the minimum capital requirements have been increased under *Basel III*. The Tier I capital requirement which is the capital a bank needs to have to absorb short term losses has been increased to 7 percent. The overall capital adequacy requirement which is a measure of total (Tier I + Tier II) capital as a function of risk weighted assets has now been increased to 9 percent.

2.8.2.2 Leverage

As banks take on more risk, their exposed assets increase. *Basel III* requires that banks have adequate capital to cover their risk exposure. Hence the leverage ratio which is expressed as a function of Tier I capital to the total consolidated assets of the bank must equal or exceed 3 percent under *Basel III* norms.

2.8.2.2 Liquidity

Under *Basel III* norms banks are required to have adequate liquidity. Banks are required to have adequate amounts of high quality liquid assets to cover their cash outflows. Thus the Liquidity Coverage Ratio (LCR) of banks, which is a measure of high quality liquid assets as a function of the cash outflows over 30 days, must be equal to or greater than 100 percent as per *Basel III* norms.

2.8.2.3 Implication for Indian Banks

The RBI introduced Basel norms to the Indian banking space in 2003. It expects all banks to be fully compliant with *Basel III* norms by March 2019. Indian banks will have to significantly increase capital, leverage and liquidity amid an environment of deteriorating asset quality which will be a major challenge. This could result in reduced lending and lower profitability for India's banks. Meeting LCR requirements amidst strict CRR and SLR requirements from the RBI will not prove easy for Indian banks.

2.9 Recent Trends in Indian Banking

In the last 5 years the Indian banking landscape has undergone a dramatic transformation. 23 new banking licenses were granted by the RBI towards the setting up of universal banks, payment banks and small finance banks to promote financial inclusion. Universal banks are required to target 40 percent of their lending activity to priority sectors thereby fostering financial inclusion. Payments banks can accept deposits up to Rs. 1 lakh per customer, issue debit cards, provide remittance services and distribute mutual fund and insurance products. Small finance banks provide banking activities to small business units, farmers, micro and small industries and even the unorganized sector.

Additionally with the demonetization activity carried out by the government at the end of 2016, digital payment technologies and online wallets such as Paytm, Freecharge and Mobikwik have gained in popularity. Mobile banking has also seen an upsurge as has the usage of credit and debit cards. This has also brought cyber security issues to the forefront and the need for secure authentication processes for transactions.

2.10 Measures of Bank Profitability

There are several key measures of bank profitability. Among the most widely measures of bank profitability are the Return on Assets (ROA), The Return on Equity (ROE) and The Net Interest Margin.

2.10.1 Return on Assets (ROA)

The ROA is the most widely used measure of bank profitability. It shows how profitable a bank is relative to its total asset base. The ROA of a bank indicates how efficient the bank's management is in deploying the bank's entire asset base to generate profits. The benchmark ROA is about 1 percent for banks globally. While banks must exceed their industry benchmark ROA, too high an ROA would imply that they are not reinvesting in assets for their future and must be taken as a warning sign.

2.10.2 Return on Equity (ROE)

The ROE is widely followed by investors. It shows how profitable a bank is relative to its equity base. The ROE of a bank indicates how well the banks management deploys share holder funds to generate profits. In other words the ROE of a bank gives you the returns for each dollar invested in it. Higher the ROE better the bank. Investors in banks tend to look for banks whose ROE shows an increasing trend over time.

2.10.3 Net Interest Margin (NIM)

The NIM of a bank is the difference between the interest income earned by a bank and the interest paid by it expressed as a function of its interest earning assets. Higher the NIM more profitable will be the banks. Additionally banks with improving asset quality will have increasing NIM's. The NIM of a bank is an indicator of the effectiveness of a bank's investment decisions.

2.11 Determinants of Bank Profitability

There are several important determinants of bank profitability. These include both internal and external determinants. Internal determinants of profitability include asset size and measures of capital adequacy, asset quality, liquidity, operating efficiency and financial risk. External determinants of bank profitability include macroeconomic determinants such as the gross domestic product (GDP) growth rate and the annual inflation rate.

2.12 Current Scenario in Indian Banking

The banking system in India consists of a mix of public, private, regional rural and foreign banks. Below is a look at some key issues and challenges that have emerged in the last five years in bank asset quality and credit growth:

2.12.1 Asset Quality

Asset quality is a very key metric of the banking sector and is an important benchmark of bank lending. We can measure this by the growth in non-performing assets. The figure below summarizes the growth in non-performing assets in the five quarters between June 2016 and June 2017:

Figure 2.4: Quarterly Growth in Non-Performing Assets (NPA's) of Indian Banks

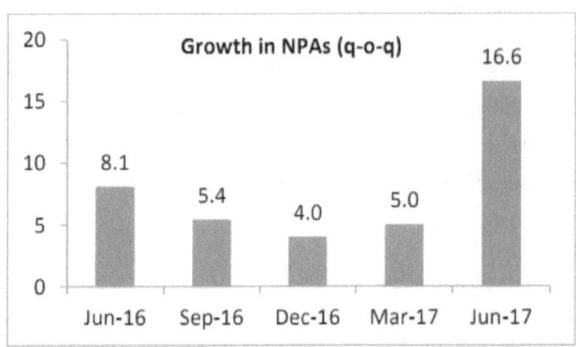

Source: Zee Business

As can be seen in Figure 2.4 NPA growth has spiked recently as asset quality has deteriorated across the banking sector. Public sector banks were the hardest hit in this regard and faced significant challenges in their asset quality when compared to their private sector counterparts as can be seen below in Figure 2.5:

Figure 2.5: Gross NPA Levels at Top Indian Banks

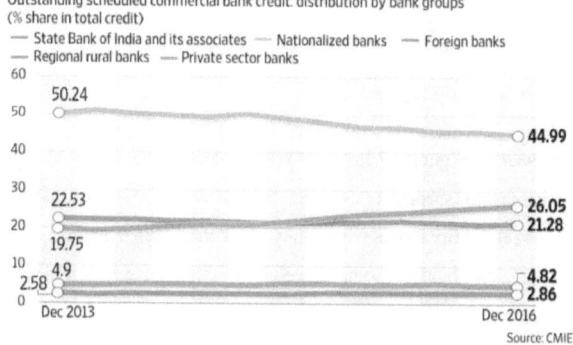

Source: VCCIRCLE.com

2.12.2 Percentage Share in Total Credit

The lending activity of the different banks over a three-year period from December 2013 to December 2016 as measured by the share of total credit is presented below in Figure 2.6:

Figure 2.6: Percentage Share in Total Credit for Different Indian Bank Groups

Outstanding scheduled commercial bank credit: distribution by bank groups
(% share in total credit)
— State Bank of India and its associates — Nationalized banks — Foreign banks
— Regional rural banks — Private sector banks

Dec 2013	Dec 2016
50.24	44.99
22.53	26.05
19.75	21.28
4.9	4.82
2.58	2.86

Source: CMIE

While the percentage share of nationalized public sector banks is still higher than that of other banks, public sector banks have experienced a steady decline in their lending activity. Meanwhile private sector banks have seen a steady uptick in lending activity. This could be largely a result of the asset quality issues that have been plaguing the Indian banking sector in general and public sector banks in particular.

2.12.3 Growth in Advances

Another key metric for banks is loan growth. Figure 2.7 summarizes the growth in advances for the sector for the three-year period between 2013 and 2016:

Figure 2.7: Growth in Advances for Different Indian Bank Groups

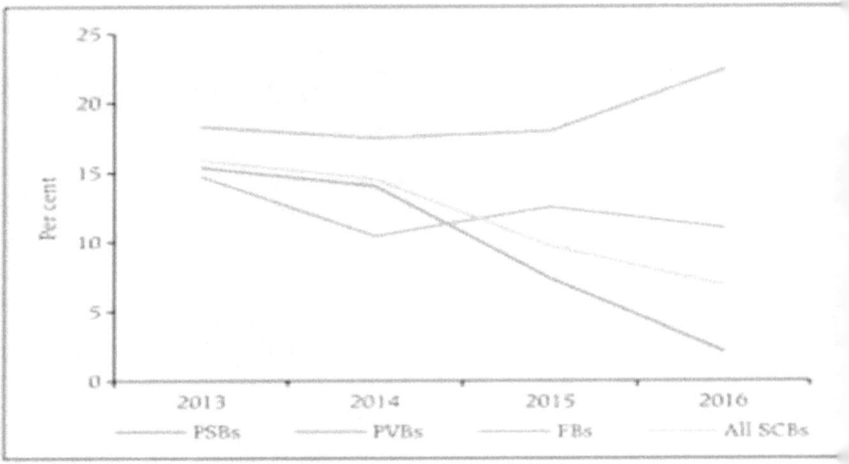

Source: Banks' annual accounts.

As can be seen in Figure 2.7 loan growth has decelerated for most banks over the last three years. This is not surprising as banks have grown a bit more cautious with their lending given the asset quality issues which they are facing. However, an exception to this has been the private sector banks who have seen a growth in advances. This is mainly due to the fact that private banks have managed to maintain and improve their asset quality when compared to their other counterparts.

2.12.4 Percentage Share in Total Assets and Profits

Figure 2.8 shows the percentage asset share and the percentage profit share of the respective bank groups over a three-year period from 2014 to 2016:

Figure 2.8: Percentage Share in Total Assets and Profits for Different Indian Bank Groups

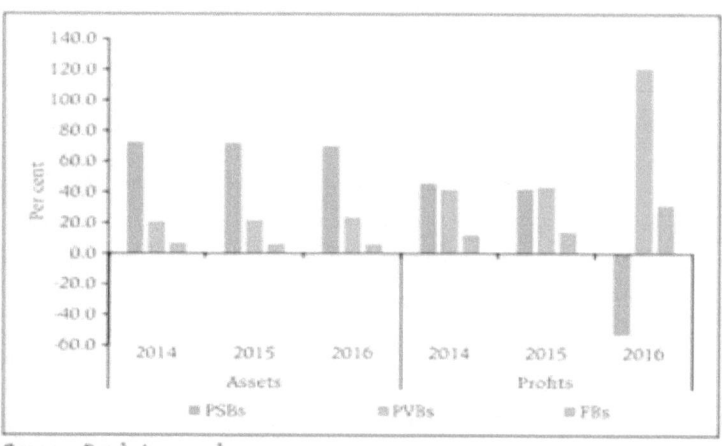

Source: Banks' annual accounts.

While the percentage share of total assets of public sector banks is much higher than their private and foreign counterparts, the asset share of public banks seems to have reached a point of saturation and is no longer growing. Private sector banks on the other hand have seen a steady increase in their asset share, while foreign banks have seen moderate increases in asset share. When it comes to share of profits, the profit share of private sector banks has exponentially increased over the last three years. Foreign banks have also seen their share in profits increase significantly. This has come at the expense of public sector banks whose share in profits has dramatically decreased.

Thus the Indian banking sector seems rather fragile with rapidly deteriorating asset quality, declining credit growth and declining share in assets and profits with only a handful of private sector banks showing improvement in these key metrics. Thus an assessment of profitability of these banks and the drivers of profitability can throw light on how to address these challenges and to make this critically important sector of the economy more robust.

2.13 Operational Definitions

Of the variables chosen for the study, bank size as measured by stock market capitalization is a key bank metric that shows how large the bank is. The capital adequacy ratio is a measure of capital adequacy that tells you if the bank has adequate amounts of capital to cover its risk exposure. The percentage net Non-Performing Assets (NPAs) is a measure of asset quality at banks. Higher NPAs would imply lower asset quality.

Business per employee is an indicator that measure productivity of the bank's work force. Interest income to average working funds and noninterest income to average working funds are key income measures that indicate the ability of the bank to generate different streams of income from funds at its disposal. Of the dependent variables chosen for the study, the Return on Assets (ROA) and the Return on Equity (ROE) are measures of the bank's profitability as a function of the bank's asset base and equity. Higher the ROA and ROE, greater would be the bank's profitability.

CHAPTER 3

REVIEW OF LITERATURE

CHAPTER III

REVIEW OF LITERATURE

There are several studies that have examined the profitability of banks both in India and in other countries. This chapter provides a review of major studies undertaken on the banking sector in India and in other countries. This chapter is organized into three sub sections. The first sub section looks at banking studies in the global context. The second sub section look at key banking studies in India. The third sub section is a summary of some important studies reviewed in this chapter. The research gap identified is described in the last sub section.

There are several factors that impact the profitability of banks (**Sufian and Habibullah, (2010)**; **Dietrich and Wanzenried, (2011)**). These factors can be broadly classified as either **internal determinants** that originate within the firm such as bank size, capital, risk management, expenses management, and diversification (**Molyneux and Thornton, (1992)**; **Goddard et al., (2004)**; **Bodla and Verma, (2006)**) or **external determinants** that are outside the firm like market concentration, industry size and ownership, inflation, interest rates, money supply and Gross Domestic Product (GDP) (**Zarrouk et al., (2016)**; **Chirwa, (2003)**).

3.1 Studies in the Global Context

Sufian, (2009) examined the determinants of Malaysian domestic and foreign commercial bank profitability during the period 2000-2004. The independent bank specific variables used in the study were: total loans to total assets, logarithm of total assets, loans loss provisions to total loans, non-interest income to total assets, total overhead expenses to total assets, and book value of stockholder's equity. The profitability measure ROA served as the dependent variable.

It was found that Malaysian banks having exposure to higher credit risk and loan concentration exhibit lower profitability levels. Additionally, banks that have a higher level of capitalization, higher proportion of income from noninterest sources, and high operational expenses proved to be relatively more profitable.

Godard et al., (2004) studied a sample of 583 commercial, savings, and co-operative banks from five major European Union countries during the mid-1990s. Here the vector auto regression (VAR) model was used to study the relationship between the return on equity, logarithmic size and logarithmic growth of the banks. Their study found that banks that maintain a high capital to assets ratio grew at a modest rate, with their growth being linked to prevailing macroeconomic conditions. Their study also found a positive relationship between concentration and bank profitability.

Chronopoulos et al., (2013) studied a sample of US banks from 1984 to 2010. Here bank profitability as determined by the Return on Assets (ROA) is modeled as a function of regulatory factors, industry and economy wide factors and bank specific factors. Their study found size, diversification, liquidity, credit risk and asset growth significantly influenced bank profitability. Profits were found to be cyclical in nature and tended to increase during phases of economic growth and fell during periods of slow growth. The great recession of 2008 was found to increase the persistence of bank profitability following regulations directed at stabilizing the banking system.

Sufian and Habibullah, (2010) examined the profitability of Indonesian banks during the period from 1990 to 2005. The independent bank specific variables used in the study were: total loans divided to total assets, logarithm of total assets, loans loss provisions to total loans, non- interest income to total assets, total overhead expenses to total assets, and book value of stockholders equity. The profitability measure ROA served as the dependent variable.

Their study found that income diversification and capitalization were positively related to bank profitability, while size and overhead costs impacted profitability negatively. They also found the Asian financial crisis of 1998 negatively impacted the profitability of the banks studied.

Growe et al, (2014) examined the influence of a wide range of determinants on profitability and performance measurement of U.S. regional banks during the period from 1994 to 2011. The dependent variables used in the study were the profitability measures ROA, ROE and changes in ROA and ROE. The independent variables taken were macroeconomic variables such as the CPI, GDP and the yield curve differential, industry specific determinants such as bank assets to GDP and stock market capitalization to bank assets and bank specific determinants such as the efficiency ratio, equity to assets, provision for credit losses, reserve for credit losses, non-performing assets, net charge offs, noninterest income to revenue, the natural logarithm of total assets, loan to assets, equity growth, equity to asset growth and cost to assets.

Their study found that the efficiency ratio and provisions for credit losses negatively impacted profitability while equity scaled by assets positively impacted profitability. Additionally the level of nonperforming assets negatively impacted profitability while macroeconomic variables had no influence on bank profitability.

Chirwa, (2003) investigated the relationship between market structure and profitability of commercial banks in Malawi using time series data between 1970 and 1994. The profitability measures used were ROA, ROE and the return on capital (ROC). These served as the dependent variables. The independent variables were the concentration ratio, the capital to asset ratio, the loan to asset ratio, the assets of commercial banks, the ratio of demand deposits to total deposits, the total banking industry deposits, and the growth of the banking industry deposits.

The analysis found a strong relationship between bank performance and concentration. A positive relationship was also observed between profitability and the loan to asset ratio. The ratio of demand deposits to total deposits was also an important determinant of commercial bank profitability.

Zarrouk et al., (2016) compared Islamic banking to conventional banking in the Middle East and North Africa (MENA) region. A sample of 51 Islamic banks was chosen for the study covering a period from 1994 to 2012. Here ROA, ROE and net profit margin served as the dependent variables. The independent variables chosen include bank specific variables such as the loans to total assets, loan loss provision to net interest revenue, loan loss reserves to gross loans, tier-1 capital ratio, asset utilization and income expense ratio, equity to total assets, equity to debt ratio, cost to income ratio, book value per share, earnings per share and the total liabilities to total assets ratio. Other independent variables chosen were macroeconomic variables such as the GDP per capita and investment and the annual inflation rate.

Their study found that Islamic bank profitability was positively affected by the cost effectiveness of banks, their asset quality and level of capitalization. The inflation rate negatively impacted Islamic bank profitability. Overall the determinants of profitability did not differ considerably for Islamic and traditional banks.

Massod and Ashraf, (2012) looked at the effect of bank specific variables such as asset size, capital adequacy, asset quality, liquidity, operating efficiency and financial risk and macroeconomic determinants such as the annual real gross domestic growth rate and the annual inflation rate on profitability as measured by the return on assets (ROA) and return on equity (ROE) of banks in 12 Islamic countries with a fixed effects panel data model.

Their study found that banks with larger asset sizes were highly profitable. Capital adequacy and the loans to assets also positively influenced profitability. Gearing was positively correlated to ROA but negatively correlated to ROE suggesting that financial risk at Islamic banks influenced ROA positively but impacted ROE negatively.

Liu and Wilson, (2010) examined the role of key determinants on the profitability of Japanese banks over the period 2000 to 2007. The measures of profitability chosen were: ROA, ROE and net interest margin (NIM). The independent variables that were chosen included bank specific and macroeconomic determinants.

The bank specific determinants chosen were: noninterest income to total operating income ratio, the loans to assets ratio, the capital to assets ratio, the cost to income ratio, the ratio of impaired loan to gross loans granted and market share. The macro economic variables chosen were the sum of the squares of each bank's market shares, the real GDP growth of Japan and the stock market capitalization relative to GDP.

Their study found that well capitalized, efficient banks, with lower credit risks tended to outperform their less capitalized, less efficient counterparts having higher credit risks. Additionally, concentration, Gross Domestic Product (GDP) growth and the extent of stock market development played an important role in determining the profitability of Japanese banks.

Sufian and Habibullah, (2009) examined internal and external determinants of profitability of the Chinese banking sector during the six-year period from 2000 to 2005. The independent bank specific variables used in the study were total loans to total assets, logarithm of total assets, loans loss provisions to total loans, noninterest income to total assets, total overhead expenses to total assets, and book value of stockholder's equity. The profitability measure ROA served as the dependent variable.

Their study found that size and costs resulted in lower commercial bank profitability. In addition, it was found the more diversified and better capitalized banks exhibited higher profitability levels. Economic growth impacted bank profitability positively while money supply growth impacted bank profitability negatively.

Tan and Floros, (2012) examined the determinants of profitability of Chinese banks. Over 100 Chinese banks were studied from 2003 to 2009. The measures of profitability used as dependent variables were: the return on assets and net interest margin. The independent variables included bank specific, industry specific and macroeconomic variables.

Bank specific variables chosen were: the log of total assets, loan loss provisions to total loans, loans to assets, tax to operating profit before tax, shareholder's equity to total assets, overhead expenses to total assets, noninterest income to gross revenues and gross revenue to number of employees. Industry specific variables included bank assets to assets of banking industry, bank assets to GDP and market capitalization of listed companies to GDP. The annual inflation rate was the macroeconomic variable chosen.

Their study found a positive relationship between bank profitability and cost efficiency, banking sector development, stock market development and inflation in China. The authors suggested that low profitability can be explained by higher volumes of non-traditional activity and higher taxation. The authors further suggested that Chinese banks must increase their productivity to boost their profitability. They also suggested that the government should gradually continue to open up the banking sector, as the development of the financial sector would help in increasing bank profits.

Miller and Noulas, (1997) studied large commercial banks in the US in the late 1980's and found that loan loss provisions and net charge offs had a significant negative effect on the profitability of large banks in the US. The net charge offs were further affected by the composition of assets and liabilities. Thus, the asset liability portfolio decisions of commercial banks affect the profitability of these institutions through net charge offs. It was also observed that higher salaries and benefits per employee were consistently associated with higher net charge offs to total assets. This suggested that banks with higher salaries and benefits would require higher net interest margins to maintain profitability.

Smirlock & Brown, (1986) studied the efficiency of key players in the US banking industry by examining the effect of concentration on bank profits. Their study found that leading firms served as price setters while secondary firms served as price takers. Their findings suggested that leading firms tended to be more efficient than their counterparts. Their study also suggested that higher profits earned by these firms were due to their efficiency and not due to the collusive behavior among the leading players.

In a study done on Tunisian banks from 1980-2000, **Ben Naceur and Goaied, (2001)** found that banks with relatively high amount of capital and overhead expenses exhibited higher net interest margins and profitability levels. Their study also found that bank size was negatively related to bank profitability. Additionally, stock market development had a positive impact on bank profitability. Further private banks were found to be relatively more profitable than their state-owned counterparts.

Using Data Envelopment Analysis (DEA), **Chu and Lim, (1998)** evaluated the relative cost and profit efficiency of six Singapore listed banks from 1992 to 1996. Average profit efficiency was found to be lower than cost efficiency for these banks. Mean profit efficiency was however higher when compared to banks in the United States and Spain. It was also found that share price performance was influenced more by changes in profit rather than cost efficiency.

Molyneux and Forbes, (1995) studied a sample of European banks from 1986 to 1989. The findings of their study showed that bank profitability was mainly influenced by market concentration. Their study pointed out that in most of the countries they studied they found that a small number of banks controlled a greater proportion of the market share. Thus, bank margins were maintained largely due to collusion and anti-competitive practices of these banks.

Ayadi and Boujelbene, (2012) examined the determinants of profitability of a sample of 12 Tunisian banks from 1995 to 2005. Here the dependent variable and the measure of profitability used was the return on average assets (ROAA). The independent variables included bank specific, financial structure and macroeconomic variables.

Bank specific variables used in the study were: the ratio of the bank credit to the total assets, the ratio of the liquid assets to the customer and short-term investment, the ratio of the book value of equity capital to total assets and total assets. The financial structure variables chosen were the ratio of the total assets of the largest banks to the total assets of all the banks, the market capitalization to GDP ratio, the market capitalization to total assets and the total assets to GDP. The macroeconomic variables chosen were the real growth of GDP and the annual inflation rate.

It was found that bank capitalization and the size of the bank have a positive effect on bank profitability. Additionally, the financial structure ratios of bank assets to GDP and stock market capitalization to banking assets had a negative effect on bank profitability. Macroeconomic indicators however did not influence bank profitability.

Dietrich and G. Wanzenried, (2011) analyzed the determinants of profitability of 453 commercial banks in Switzerland during the period from 1999 to 2008. The return on average assets (ROAA) and the return on average equity (ROAE) were the profitability measures that served as dependent variables in the study.

The independent variables included bank specific, industry specific and macroeconomic variables. Bank specific variables used in the study were the equity over total assets, cost-income ratio, loan loss provisions over total loans, yearly growth of deposits, difference between bank and market growth of total loans, bank size as measured by total assets, interest income share, funding costs, bank age, bank ownership and nationality. Industry specific and macroeconomic variables chosen include the effective tax rate, yearly change of regional population, real GDP growth, term structure of interest rate, stock market capitalization and market structure.

It was found that the capital ratio positively impacted ROAA but negatively impacted ROAE. The efficiency measure, cost to income ratio negatively impacted profitability. The loan loss provisions relative to total loans ratio, which is a measure of credit quality did not influence profitability. The yearly growth of deposits also did not influence bank profitability. It was also found that larger commercial banks had slightly less ROAA than medium-sized banks but this was not the case when ROAE was used as the profitability measure. Additionally, banks with a higher share of interest income relative to the total income were significantly less profitable.

Funding costs did not have a significant impact on ROAA. Newer banks were slightly more profitable than older banks. Privately banks were more profitable than state owned banks. Taxation negatively affected bank profitability. The yearly change of the regional population positively influenced bank profitability. The GDP growth rate did not affect bank profitability. However, the term structure of interest rates positively influenced bank profitability. The stock market capitalization had a positive impact on bank profitability while market structure did not influence bank profitability.

Garza-Garcia (2012) studied Mexican banks from 2001 to 2009. He found that market share was a main determinant of bank profitability in Mexico. He also found that bank profits persist over time suggesting that the banking sector is not competitive. There was no relationship between efficiency and bank profits. It was found that capitalization levels increased bank profits while the threat of liquidity risk lowered profitability.

Molyneux and Thornton, (1992) studied banks in eighteen European countries between 1986 and 1989. They found a significant positive relationship between profitability as measured by the return on equity and the level of interest rates in each country. There was also a positive relationship between profitability and bank concentration. There was additionally a positive relationship between profitability and government ownership.

Holden and El-Bannany, (2004) investigated whether investment in information technology systems affects bank profitability in the UK. They found that the number of automated teller machines installed by a bank has a positive impact on bank profitability. Thus, upgrades to information technology can impact bank profitability.

Ghauri, (2014) looked at 15 banks listed on the Karachi stock exchange during the period from 2008 to 2011. The study used regression analysis and studied the effect of size, dividend yield, the return on assets and asset growth on the share price. It found that bank size had a significant positive relationship with the share price while the other variables did not have a significant relationship with the banks share price.

Uddin, (2009) studied the impact of micro and macroeconomic factors on share price performance of bank leasing and insurance companies in the Dhaka stock exchange in Bangladesh through multiple regression analysis. It was found that a linear relationship existed between market returns and some microeconomic factors such as net asset value per share, dividend percentage, and earnings per share. There was no relationship however between market returns and macroeconomic factors studied.

Beccalli et al., (2006) studied the relationship between cost efficiency and share price performance of selected European Banks. Their study found that changes in operating efficiency influenced changes in stock prices more than the influence of key financial ratios. Their study also found that share price performance as measured by annual stock returns of cost efficient banks was significantly better than their inefficient peers.

Menaje, (2012) looked at the impact of variables such as Earnings per Share (EPS) and the return on assets on the share prices of 10 publicly listed banks in the Philippines in 2009 with a multiple regression analysis. It was found that the Earnings per Share had a strong positive correlation with the share prices while the return on assets had a weak negative correlation with the share price.

Seetharaman and Raj, (2011) studied the impact of Earnings per share (EPS) and earnings announcements on the share price performance of a public Malaysian bank. Their study found a very strong positive correlation between the Bank's EPS and share price. Their study also found earnings announcements had a significant impact on the share price of the bank.

Ali and Chowdhury, (2010) examined reactions of stock prices of listed Private Commercial Banks (PCBs) in Bangladesh following 44 days of the dividend announcements. Their study found that stock price reactions to dividend announcements were not material. Dividend announcements did not appear to disseminate any information due to the presence of insider trading in the stock market and other over riding factors in the capital market.

3.2 Studies in the Indian Context

Ganesan, (2001) studied a wide range of public sector banks in India for a period of four years. Here profitability as measured by net profit or net profit as a function of total assets is modeled as a function of several key bank input and output factors. Among those it was found that interest cost, interest income, other income, deposits per branch and credit to total assets were some of the key determinants of profitability of these banks.

Bodla and Verma, (2006) studied the impact of several key variables on net profit for a sample of 27 public banks in India over a period of 13 years starting from the financial year 1991-92 through a multiple regression analysis. The variables chosen were the interest spread, noninterest income, the credit to deposit ratio, the percentage NPA, provision and contingencies, operating expenses, business per employee and profit per employee. Their study found that noninterest income, operating expenses, provision and contingencies and spread had a significant relationship with net profits.

Dhanabhakyam and Kavitha, (2012) focused on six public sector banks from 2001-2010 and studied the relationship between selected internal determinants. The independent variables chosen were: the credit deposit ratio, total investment to total deposits, interest income to working funds, spread to working funds, noninterest income to working funds and noninterest expenses to working funds. Net Profit to Working Fund was the dependent variable. Their study found that the credit deposit ratio and noninterest income to working funds were correlated to net profit to working funds for most banks. Thus these variables proved to be useful determinants of profitability of the banks studied.

Singh, (2006) examined the relationship between key financial and bank specific indicators and stock prices of selected Indian Banks. The financial indicators chosen were Profit after Tax, PAT to Total Assets, PAT to Operating Income and Return on Net Worth. The bank specific indicators chosen were Profit to Employee, Noninterest Income to Total Funds and NPA to Total Advances. All financial indicators showed a positive correlation with stock prices as did Profit per Employee. The NPA to Total Advances ratio showed a negative relationship with stock prices.

Sensarma and Jayadev, (2009) examined the effect of different types of risk namely credit, hedge and interest rate risk on the Return on Equity (ROE) of private and public banks in India from 1998-2006. Their study found that the ROE is sensitive to the risk management capability of banks. It was found that risk management capabilities of Indian banks had been improving over time. The authors suggest that banks that attempt to enhance shareholder value have to focus on successfully managing various underlying risks. Thus shareholders will stick with banks that are better risk managers.

Thiagarajan et al., (2011) studied the determinants of profitability of select public and private sector banks from 2000 to 2010. Their study found that the cost of borrowing and net NPA's had a significant negative correlation with profitability for public sector banks. Additionally return on investments, return on advances and operating profit showed a positive correlation with profitability for both public and private sector banks. Their study also found that the return on investments and return on advances exerted a significant influence on the profitability of private sector banks.

Vyas et al., (2008) studied the impact of bank specific factors like, capital to risk weighted assets ratio, non-interest income and net interest margin on bank profitability as measured by the return on assets of scheduled commercial banks in India through a panel data framework from 1997-2007. All the factors studied had a positive impact on bank profitability. There were also no significant differences between the profitability of public sector banks, private sector banks and foreign banks operating in India.

3.3 Summary of Key Determinants of Profitability and Profitability Measures used in Select Research Studies

The important determinants of bank profitability and profitability measures identified in the literature from studies described in the previous sections are summarized below in table 3.1:

Table 3.1 Determinants of Bank Profitability

Determinant	Measure	Profitability Measures	Type	Study
Bank Credit / Total Assets	Bank Specific	The Return on Average Assets	Internal	Ayadi, & Boujelbene, (2012)
Market Capitalization / Total Assets	Financial Structure	The Return on Average Assets	Internal	Ayadi, & Boujelbene, (2012)
Annual Inflation Rate	Macroeconomic	The Return on Average Assets	External	Ayadi, & Boujelbene, (2012)
Capital / Total Assets	Risk	The Return on Assets The Return on Equity The Return on Capital	Internal	Chirwa, (2003)
Demand Deposits / Total Deposits	Cost of Funds	The Return on Assets The Return on Equity The Return on Capital	Internal	Chirwa, (2003)
Total Deposits	Market Size	The Return on Assets The Return on Equity The Return on Capital	Internal	Chirwa, (2003)
Equity / Total Assets	Bank Specific	The Return on Average Assets The Return on Average Equity	Internal	Dietrich & Wanzenried, (2011).
Real GDP Growth	Macroeconomic	The Return on Average Assets The	External	Dietrich & Wanzenried, (2011).

		Return on Average Equity		
Effective Tax Rate	Macroeconomic	The Return on Average Assets The Return on Average Equity	External	Dietrich & Wanzenried, (2011).
Loan Loss Provisions / Total Loans	Credit Risk	The Return on Assets	Internal	Sufian, (2009)
Noninterest Income over Total Assets	Non-Traditional Activities	The Return on Assets	Internal	Sufian, (2009)
Book Value of Stock-Holders' Equity as a Fraction of Total Assets	Capital Structure	The Return on Assets	Internal	Sufian, (2009)
Yield Curve	Macroeconomic	The Return on Assets The Return on Equity Change in The Return on Assets Change in The Return on Equity	External	Growe et al., (2014)
Stock Market Capitalization / Total Assets	Industry Specific	The Return on Assets The Return on Equity Change in The Return on Assets	Internal	Growe et al., (2014)

		Change in The Return on Equity		
Noninterest Expense / Total Income	Bank Specific	The Return on Assets The Return on Equity Change in The Return on Assets Change in The Return on Equity	Internal	Growe et al., (2014)

3.4 Conclusion

While several studies till date have looked at some key determinants of bank profitability and their impact on bank profitability, very few studies have compared the effect of key determinants on profitability of a larger cross section of banks that represent the banking sector as a whole. Hence an attempt has been made in this study to know the key drivers of profitability of the banking sector in India by selecting a wider cross section of banks. The study also looks at the similarities or the differences of the influence of selected determinants on two different profitability measures across the sample of banks selected for research.

CHAPTER 4

RESEARCH METHODOLOGY

CHAPTER IV

RESEARCH METHODOLOGY

The current study was conducted based on secondary data. It was a descriptive study and involved empirical research. Data from bank financial statements has been used for the analysis. The collected data has been subjected to relevant statistical tests for the purpose of analysis. Forecasting models have been attempted in the study. These aspects are dealt with in this chapter.

4.1 Conceptual Frame Work of the Study

Based on the profitability measures and key determinants of bank profitability used in other studies discussed in chapter III, this study looked at the impact of some key internal determinants on the profitability of forty listed commercial banks in India comprising of both private and public sector banks. The conceptual framework of the study is shown in figure 4.1:

Figure 4.1: Conceptual Framework of the Study

——— Measures Addressed in the Study
- - - - - Measures Not Addressed in the Study

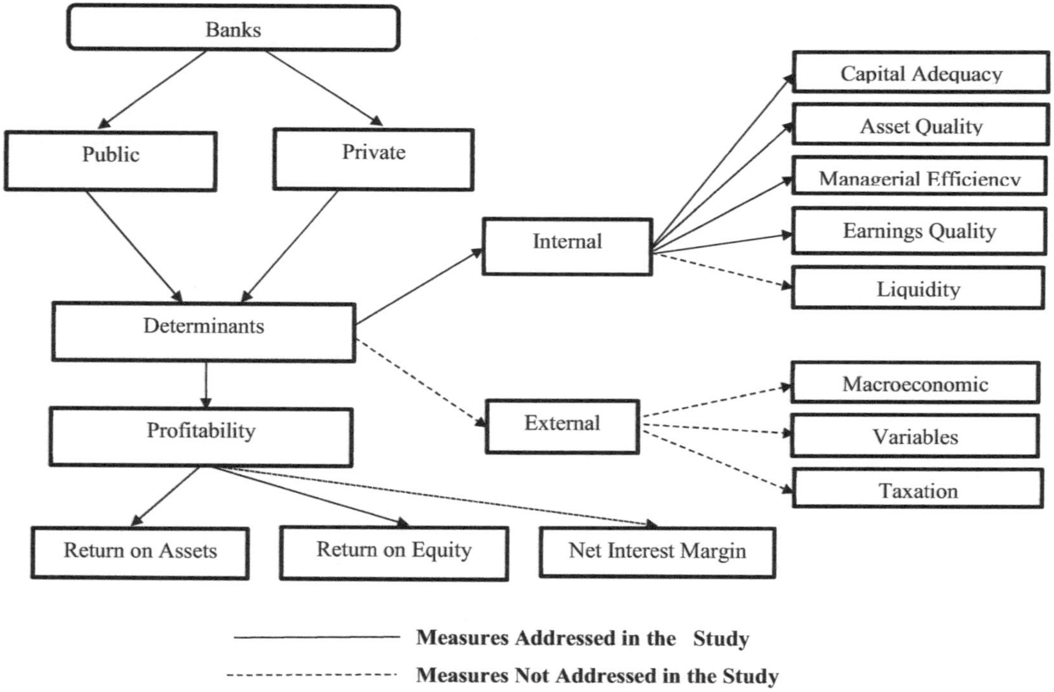

The profitability measures used were the return on assets (ROA) and the return on equity (ROE). The determinants of profitability selected were a key bank metric the bank size as measured by market capitalization, a lending measure the deposit to credit ratio (DCR), two income measures that reflect earnings quality which were the interest income to average working funds (IIAWF) and noninterest income to average working funds (NIIAWF) which is a measure of fee based income, a productivity measure the business per employee (BPE) which is also a measure of managerial efficiency, a measure of capital adequacy the capital adequacy ratio (CAR) and a measure of asset quality the percentage net non-performing assets (NNPA).

4.2 Research Design

The research design used was a descriptive research design that involved empirical research. It involved quantitative analysis of the data. The current research design encompasses the variables used, the data to be collected and the plan of analysis to be followed.

4.2.1 Variables Selected

The variables were selected after evaluating key income and cost drivers of banks. These are discussed below;

4.2.1.1 Income and Cost Components of Banks

To understand the drivers of bank profitability the income and cost structure of banks is very important. Figure 4.2 illustrates the income and cost structure of banks:

Figure 4.2: Income and Cost Components of Banks

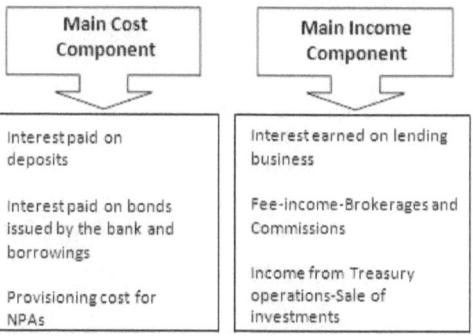

Source: Imsindia.com

4.2.1.1.1 Income Components of Banks

The primary source of income for most Indian banks is interest income. This accounts for well over 80 percent of bank incomes. Other than interest income banks generate income from fee-based sources. These include income from brokerage and commissions and also income from treasury operations and other banking activities.

4.2.1.1.2 Cost Components of Banks

The major cost incurred by a bank is the interest bank owe on their deposits. In addition banks may also incur additional interest expenses on any bonds issued by them or any other borrowings they have made. Another major cost incurred by banks is the provisioning they have to make for nonperforming assets. In the face of deteriorating asset quality across banks this has become a major cost driver for banks.

4.2.1.2 Key Variables

A variable is something that changes its value frequently and can be measured. An independent variable is one which is unaffected by other variables while a dependent variable is affected by changes in the independent variable. The following variables have been selected for the study:

Independent Variables:

A Key Bank Metric – The bank size (S), as measured by stock market capitalization.

A Key Lending Measure - The deposit to credit ratio (DCR)

Income Measures - Interest income to average working funds (IIAWF) and Noninterest income to average working funds (NIIAWF), which is a measure of fee based income,

A Productivity Measure – The business per employee (BPE)

A Measure of Capital Adequacy - The capital adequacy ratio (CAR) and

A Measure of Asset Quality – The percentage net non-performing assets (NNPA)

Dependent Variables:

Bank Profitability as measured by the Return on Assets (ROA) and the Return on Equity (ROE)

4.2.1.2.1 Bank Size

The bank size is determined by stock market capitalization. It is simply calculated as:

Bank Size = Stock Market Capitalization = Current Stock Price x Number of Shares Outstanding

4.2.1.2.2 Deposit Credit Ratio

This ratio is a key lending measure. It indicates how much deposits a bank has as a function of the loans advanced. In other words it shows how much of the mobilized funds are used for the bank's core lending activity. A lower ratio indicates the bank's dependence on deposits as a source for lending and vice-versa. A very high ratio indicates banks are not making full use of the resources at their disposal. A very low ratio is considered a warning sign and may have direct implications in deteriorating asset quality. It is calculated as:

Deposit Credit Ratio = (Total Deposits / Total Advances) x100

4.2.1.2.3 Interest Income to Average Working Funds

This ratio is a measure of a bank's core income generation activity. Banks predominantly generate income through interest on loans and advances. This ratio indicates the extent to which a bank generates income as a function of its available funds. A healthy interest income percentage is mandatory for banks. However if this ratio is too high, it could indicate the absence of diversification in the banks income stream. Too low a ratio would imply that the banks operations are hindered and would serve as a warning sign. The interest income to average working funds is calculated as:

Interest Income to Average Working Funds = (Interest Income / Average Working Funds) x100

4.2.1.2.4 Noninterest Income to Average Working Funds

This ratio is a measure of income diversification. It looks at the proportion of income generated from income other than interest income as a function of the available funds. Noninterest income consists of primarily fees, brokerage commissions and income from treasury operations. This serves to provide diversification to the banks traditional interest income stream. A higher ratio indicates better income diversification. The noninterest income to average working funds is calculated as:

Noninterest Income to

Average Working Funds = (Noninterest Income / Average Working Funds) x100

4.2.1.2.5 Business per Employee

The business per employee is also a productivity measure and measures the business generated by each employee on an average. The primary business of a bank is obtaining deposits and sanctioning loans. A rising trend in this ratio would imply that management is able to generate more business from its employees which in turn is an indication of managerial efficiency. It is calculated as:

Business per Employee = (Deposit + Advances) / Number of Employees

4.2.1.2.6 Capital Adequacy Ratio

The capital adequacy ratio is a measure of capital as a function of risk weighted assets at the bank. The capital required is a sum of Tier 1 and Tier 2 capital. Tier 1 capital is a capital buffer for short term losses while Tier 2 capital is a buffer required in the event of insolvency. The ratio indicates whether the bank is adequately capitalized to absorb operational losses. As per Basel III norms, the RBI requires Indian banks to have a capital adequacy ratio of at least 9 percent. It is calculated as:

Capital Adequacy Ratio = [Tier 1 Capital + Tier 2 Capital] x100 / Risk Weighted Assets

4.2.1.2.7 The Percentage Net NPA to Net Advances

This ratio is a widely used measure of asset quality and looks at the proportion of net nonperforming assets as a function of the advances made by the bank. Higher the ratio lower will be the asset quality. Banks need to monitor their loans and reduce nonperforming assets to improve their asset quality. It is calculated as:

Percentage Net NPA = (Net NPA's / Total Advances) x100

4.2.1.2.8 Return on Assets (ROA)

The ROA is the most widely used measure of bank profitability. It shows how profitable a bank is relative to its total asset base. The ROA of a bank indicates how efficient the bank's management is in deploying the bank's entire asset base to generate profits. The benchmark ROA is about 1 percent for banks globally. While banks must exceed their industry benchmark ROA, too high an ROA would imply that they are not reinvesting in assets for their future and must be taken as a warning sign. It is calculated as:

ROA = (Net Income / Total Assets) x100

4.2.1.2.9 Return on Equity (ROE)

The ROE is widely followed by investors. It shows how profitable a bank is relative to its equity base. The ROE of a bank indicates how well the banks management deploys share holder funds to generate profits. In other words the ROE of a bank gives you the returns for each dollar invested in it. Higher the ROE better the bank. Investors in banks tend to look for banks whose ROE shows an increasing trend over time. It is calculated as:

ROE = (Net Income / Common Equity) x100

4.2.2 Development of Working Hypothesis

When a hypothetical relationship is tested using scientific methods, it is called a research hypothesis. The research hypothesis is a predictive statement which seeks to establish the relationship between variables. Thus for a valid research hypothesis there must be at least two variables whose relationship the hypothesis seeks to establish, one independent and the other dependent (Kothari and Garg, (2014)). This study developed 14 working hypotheses between 2 dependent variables and 7 independent variables.

4.2.2.1 Null Hypothesis and Alternative Hypothesis

In statistical analysis there are two types of hypotheses involved. One is the null hypothesis and the other the alternate hypothesis. An alternative hypothesis is the hypothesis which a researcher tries to prove or accept, whereas the null hypothesis is the hypothesis that the researcher tries to disprove or reject (Kothari and Garg, (2014)).

4.2.2.2 Working Hypothesis

In line with those above objectives the following research hypotheses are chosen:

1) H_0 – Bank profitability as measured by the return of assets (ROA) does not vary with bank size

H_1 – Bank profitability as measured by ROA varies with bank size

2) H_0 – Bank profitability as measured by the return on equity (ROE) does not vary with bank size

H_1 – Bank profitability as measured by ROE varies with bank size

3) H_0 – ROA does not vary with the deposit to credit ratio

H_1 – ROA varies with the deposit to credit ratio

4) H_0 – ROE does not vary with the deposit to credit ratio

H_1 – ROE varies with the deposit to credit ratio

5) H_0 – ROA does not vary with interest income to average working funds

H_1 – ROA varies with interest income to average working funds

6) H_0 – ROE does not vary with interest income to average working funds

H_1 – ROE varies with interest income to average working funds

7) H_0 – ROA does not vary with noninterest income to average working funds

H_1 – ROA varies with noninterest income to average working funds

8) H_0 – ROE does not vary with noninterest income to average working funds

H_1 – ROE varies with noninterest income to average working funds

9) H_0 – ROA does not vary with business per employee

H_1 – ROA varies with business per employee

10) H_0 – ROE does not vary with business per employee

H_1 – ROE varies with business per employee

11) H_0 – ROA does not vary with the capital adequacy ratio

H_1 – ROA varies with the capital adequacy ratio

12) H_0 – ROE does not vary with the capital adequacy ratio

H_1 – ROE varies with the capital adequacy ratio

13) H_0 – ROA does not vary with the percentage Net NPA

H_1 – ROA varies with the percentage Net NPA

14) H_0 – ROE does not vary with the percentage Net NPA

H_1 – ROE varies with the percentage Net NPA

4.2.3 Sample Design

The sample design consists of the sampling frame, the sampling technique used and the sample description.

4.2.3.1 Sampling Frame

The RBI's data base on the Indian Economy and company financial statements were used as the sampling frame for this study. The RBI's data base on the Indian Economy is a comprehensive data base that contains detailed information on all the variables used in the study since the early 1990's. All relevant data from the financial years ending March 2006 to March 2017 was extracted from company reports and verified with the help of the RBI database.

4.2.3.2 Sampling Technique

The convenience sampling technique was broadly used while selecting the sample. All listed public and private sector banks that have been listed for a period of at least 5 years in the period between 2006 and 2015 were considered for the study.

4.2.3.3 Sample Description

The sample consisted of 40 listed commercial banks in India. Of these 24 were listed public sector banks which are summarized in Table 4.1 and 16 were listed private sector banks as indicated in Table 4.2.

Table 4.1: Sample of Public Sector Banks Chosen

S. No	Bank	Market Capitalization (Rs. Crores)	Net Interest Income (Rs. Crores)	Net Profit (Rs. Crores)	Total Assets (Rs. Crores)
1	State Bank of India	213163.77	175518.24	10484.1	2705966.3
2	Bank of Baroda	33518.69	42199.93	1383.13	694875.41
3	Punjab National Bank	20635.28	47995.76	-12282.82	720330.55
4	IDBI Bank	18641.95	27791.37	-5158.14	361767.9
5	Central Bank	17633.28	24035.51	-5104.91	333401.95
6	Canara Bank	17282.58	41252.09	-4222.24	583519.45
7	Bank of India	16288.13	39290.87	-1558.34	626309.27
8	Indian Bank	14435.17	17113.65	1258.99	218233.15
9	Union Bank	9728.37	32748	-5247.37	452704.45
10	Indian Overseas Bank	7825.23	19718.61	-3416.74	247167.49
11	Vijaya Bank	7642.31	12589.84	727.02	154881.58
12	Syndicate Bank	6136.79	21775.95	-3222.84	299073.34

13	State Bank of Bikaner	5402.95	9592.47	850.6	110336.27
14	Oriental Bank	4771.07	17398.89	-5871.74	253064.72
15	State Bank of Travancore	4328.47	9608.88	337.73	114506.78
16	UCO Bank	4189.31	14020.13	-4436.37	231339.7
17	Corporation Bank	4188.85	19471.47	561.21	247891.04
18	Andhra Bank	4117.99	18027.42	174.34	222126.12
19	Dena Bank	3693.54	8932.23	-1923.15	129623.55
20	Bank of Maharashtra	3416.97	11096.42	-1145.65	159323.98
21	United Bank	3405	9427.91	219.51	141053.12
22	Allahabad Bank	3186.27	16358.49	-4674.37	237037.89
23	State Bank of Mysore	2909.85	7127.78	357.85	82975
24	Punjab & Sind Bank	1807.72	7948.75	-743.8	96643.44

Source: Moneycontrol.com as on 20/5/2019

Table 4.2: Sample of Private Sector Banks Chosen

S. No	Bank	Market Capitalization (Rs. Crores)	Net Interest Income (Rs. Crores)	Net Profit (Rs. Crores)	Total Assets (Rs. Crores)
1	HDFC Bank	522550.46	80241.35	17486.75	863840.2

2	Kotak Mahindra	246683.5	19748.49	4084.3	214589.96
3	ICICI Bank	183933.34	54965.89	6777.42	771791.46
4	Axis Bank	136829.08	45780.31	275.68	601467.66
5	IndusInd Bank	115848.56	17280.75	3605.99	178648.43
6	Yes Bank	79623.33	20267.42	4224.56	312445.6
7	ING Vysya Bank	19719.13	5205.22	657.85	60413.23
8	Federal Bank	16275.73	9752.86	878.85	114976.93
9	City Union Bank	12560.06	3173.79	502.77	35270.78
10	Karur Vysya Bank	7226.43	5622.35	605.98	61807.61
11	DCB Bank	5584.72	2412.99	245.34	30222.09
12	South India Bank	4632.32	6192.81	334.89	74312.15
13	Karnataka Bank	3409.42	5423.75	325.61	64126.55
14	Jamu and Kashmir Bank	2865.04	6685.8	-1632.29	82018.66

| 15 | Lakshmi Vilas Bank | 2375.62 | 2846.66 | 256.07 | 35244.71 |
| 16 | Dhanlaxmi Bank | 469.34 | 1089.05 | 12.38 | 12333.12 |

Source: Moneycontrol as on 20/5/2019

4.2.4 Collection of Data

Data represents sets of information. Data is obtained from two major sources. These are primary and secondary sources. Primary data is original data collected for the first time directly by the researcher. Secondary data is data that has been collected and published by reputed sources, which can be used by the researcher. Primary data can be collected through interviews, questionnaires and focus groups. Secondary data can be collected from journals, government records etc. This study used data from secondary sources.

4.2.4.1 Sources of Data

This study collected secondary data from published sources and databases. Published sources included company financial reports and reports from reputed financial institutions like the RBI and scholarly peer reviewed journals. Databases used to cross check collected data were the RBI's data base on the Indian economy and the Capitaline database. All variables were obtained from the above sources in the required time frame. The data obtained is organized as per the template shown in Table 4.3:

Table 4.3 Data Template

Bank	Year	S	CAR	DCR	BPE	NNPA	IIAWF	NIIAWF	ROA	ROE

4.2.5 Data Analysis

The plan for analysis is shown in Figure 4.2. Analytical techniques followed by other major studies were reviewed before the plan of analysis was finalized. Table 4.4 summarizes the analytical tools used in other studies on bank profitability:

Table 4.4 Data Analysis Techniques Used in Other Major Studies

Study	Author	Year	Research Tool Used
Factors Influencing Bank Profitability in a Developing Economy: Empirical Evidence from Malaysia	F. Sufian	2009	Regression
The Profitability of European Banks: A Cross-Sectional and Dynamic Panel Analysis	J. Goddard, P. Molyneux, and J.O.S. Wilson	2004	Panel Data Analysis
Determinants of Commercial Banks Profitability in Malawi: A Co Integration Approach	E. W. Chirwa	2003	Time Series Techniques of Co-integration
Is Islamic bank profitability driven by	H. Zarrouk, K. B. Jedidia and M. Moualhi	2016	The Generalized Method of Moments

same forces as conventional banks?			
Share performance and profit efficiency of banks in an oligopolistic market: evidence from Singapore	S.F. Chu and G. H. Lim	1998	Data Envelopment Analysis

Once the data has been collected an appropriate distribution has to be chosen. Descriptive statistics are obtained on each variable. After this the working hypotheses can be tested with the relevant statistical test. In the current study the working hypotheses were tested with descriptive statistics and correlation analysis.

To gage the impact of determinants on profitability, multiple regression analysis is performed starting with the most correlated variable. To further develop forecasts the proposed models are checked for normality in residuals, heteroskedasticity, multi-collinearity and auto correlation. The final model and forecasts were developed with the quantile regression technique. The SPSS 18.0 package and the Gretl 1.9.4 econometrics package were used to analyze the data.

Figure 4.3 Plan of Analysis

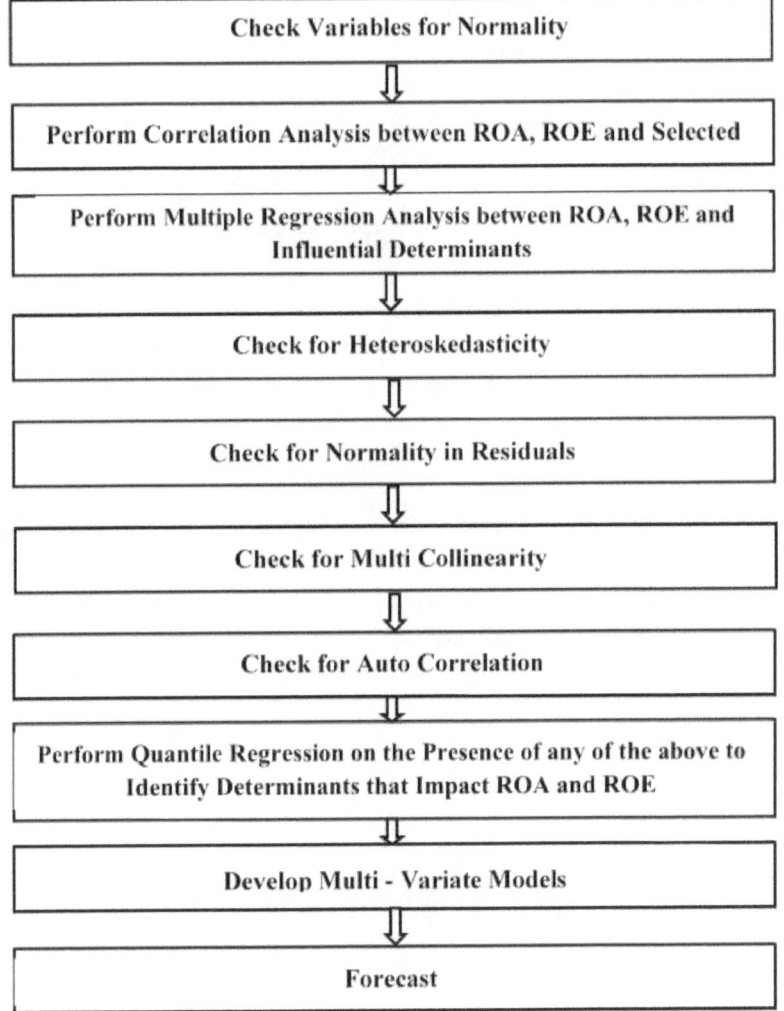

4.2.5.1 Choice of Distribution

There are several distributions to choose from. These include the binomial distribution, the Poisson distribution and the normal distribution (Damodran, 2018).

4.2.5.1.1 Binomial Distribution

The binomial distribution is a type of probability distribution which looks at the probability that a variable will assume one of two independent values under a given set of conditions. The binomial distribution assumes that there is only one outcome for every trial, the same probability of success is attributable to every trial and that every trial is mutually exclusive or independent of the other. An example of a binomial distribution is shown in figure 4.4.

Figure 4.4 Binomial Distribution

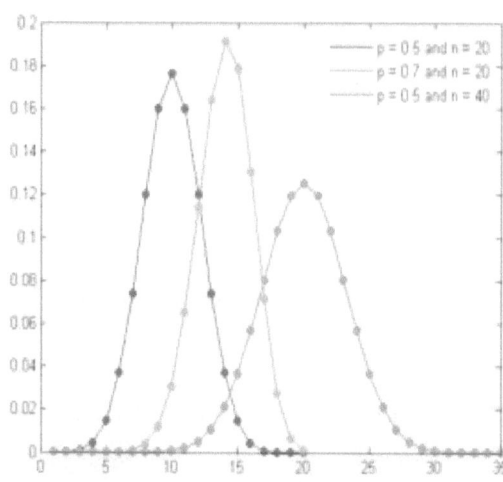

Source: Stern School of Business, New York University

4.2.5.1.2 Poisson Distribution

The Poisson distribution is a discreet probability distribution that helps in assessing the probability of an event from the frequency of its occurrence. It helps in determining the probability of a finite number of events occurring in a given interval of time. It is suitable when the sample size is large but the probability of occurrence is very low. An example of a Poisson distribution is shown in figure 4.5.

Figure 4.5 Poisson Distribution

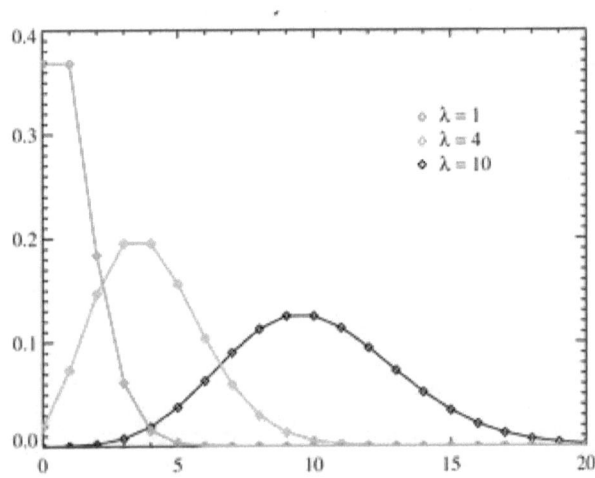

Source: Stern School of Business, New York University

4.2.5.1.3 Normal Distribution

The normal distribution is widely used and is the distribution chosen in this study. The major advantage of a normal distribution is that it is based on just two parameters the mean and standard deviation of the distribution. The probability of a value occurring can be obtained just by knowing the number of standard deviations that separate the value from the mean. The probability that a value will fall 1, 2 and 3 standard deviations from the mean is approximately 68%, 95% and 100%.

The normal curve is bell shaped and perfectly symmetrical. The distribution of the frequencies on either side of the mean is the same. The mean, median and mode of a normal are the same. Most of the variables used in this study followed a normal distribution. This was verified with Q-Q plots. An example of a normal distribution is shown in figure 4.6.

Figure 4.6 Normal Distribution

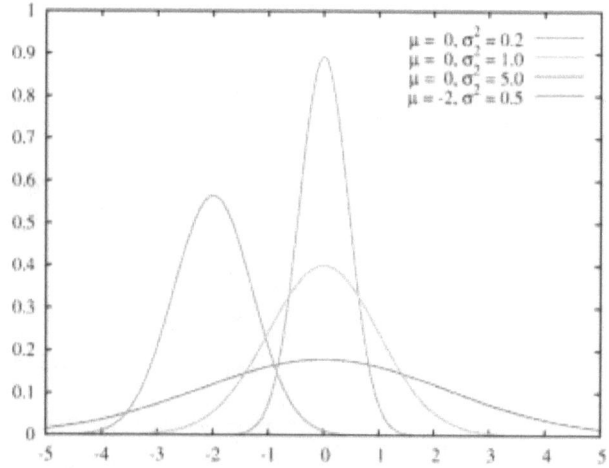

Source: Stern School of Business, New York University

4.2.5.2 Statistical Tests

Data can either be categorical or continuous. To analyze categorical data we use non parametric tests like the Chi-square test while continuous data is analyzed with parametric tests like correlation and regression. Given the range of statistical tests available, it is very important to know when a particular test can be applied. Table 4.4 summarizes variable types and the statistical tests that can be deployed:

Table 4.4 Variable Types and Statistical Tests

S. No	Independent Variable	Dependent Variable	Test	Test Outcome
1	Categorical	Categorical	Chi square, Z test	Significant difference (%)
2	Continuous	Continuous	Correlation, Regression	Significant relation
3	Categorical	Continuous	T test, ANOVA	Significant difference (mean)

Given that the data analyzed in this study is secondary in nature and continuous, Table 4.5 shows some key parametric tests that can be applied with their intended outcomes:

Table 4.5 Statistical Tests and Outcomes

Test	Outcome
Mean	Summarizing variation
T test and ANOVA	Significant difference between groups
Correlation	Significant relationship between variables
Factor Analysis	Dimension reduction and summarizing
Multiple Regression	Influence of independent variables on dependent variables
Time Series	To predict the future based on historical patterns

4.2.5.2.1 t-Test

If the sample size is small, and contains fewer than 30 data points, the t-test can be used. The t-test is used to find if there is a significant difference between the means of two groups, as long as they fit a normal distribution. Thus the t-test is a parametric test as it is contingent on the population following a normal distribution. It can be used where the standard deviation of the population is unknown. There are variations of the t-test, such as the paired sample t-test which can be used to compare performance before and after an activity such as a training program.

The t statistic is computed as:

$$t = \frac{\bar{x} - \mu_0}{s/\sqrt{n}}$$

Source: Statistics How To

Where

$\bar{x}$ = sample mean

μ_0 = population mean

s = sample standard deviation

n = sample size

4.2.5.2.2 Chi-Square Test

The t-test and several other tests are parametric tests and are contingent upon the population following a normal distribution. However many times the population may not follow a normal distribution. In such instances a non-parametric test like the chi-square test is required. The chi-square test can be run easily regardless of the distribution followed by the population. It comes in particularly handy where parametric tests cannot be used. The chi-square statistic χ^2 is computed as:

$$X^2 = \sum (O - E)^2 / E$$

Where

O = the observed frequencies and
E = the expected frequencies.

4.2.5.2.3 Analysis of Variance (ANOVA)

ANOVA is a statistical technique which is used to compare the means of two or more samples and check if they are significantly different. ANOVA is a parametric test that requires the population being tested to follow a normal distribution. The null hypothesis of ANOVA holds true when there is no difference in the means of the samples being tested.

In ANOVA the total variation is broken down into different components of variation. The sources of variations are due to controllable factors and uncontrollable factors. The variation is captured by the F statistic which is calculated as:

F = Variability between the groups / Variability within the groups

Higher the F statistic greater the chance of the alternate hypothesis being proved true, implying that there is greater chance of there being a significant difference in the means of the samples being tested. In this study F values were used to validate the statistical significance of multiple regressions performed.

4.2.5.2.4 Correlation

Correlation is a statistical test that measures the relationship between two or more variables. There is a correlation between two variables if changes in the values of a variable affect the values of the other. The two variables could move either in the same direction or in the opposite direction. However correlation does not imply causality.

Correlation was used in this study to determine the relationship between dependent and independent variables.

There is a positive correlation between two variables if they move in the same direction. This occurs when the value of one variable increases, the value of the other variable also increases and vice versa. There is a negative correlation between two variables if they move in the opposite direction. This occurs when the value of one variable increases, the value of the other variable decreases and vice versa.

4.2.5.2.4.1 Karl Pearson's Coefficient of Correlation

The Karl Pearson's Coefficient of Correlation gives a measure of the degree of correlation between two variables. For a given set of variables X and Y with N pairs of observations, the Karl Pearson's correlation coefficient r is expressed as:

$$r = \frac{n(\Sigma xy) - (\Sigma x)(\Sigma y)}{\sqrt{[n\Sigma x^2 - (\Sigma x)^2][n\Sigma y^2 - (\Sigma y)^2]}}$$

Source: Statistics How To

4.2.5.2.4.2 Spearman's Rank Correlation Coefficient

If correlation is to be established between the ranks of the variables rather than the variables themselves, the Spearman's rank correlation coefficient (ρ) is used. It is expressed as:

$$\rho = 1 - [6\Sigma D^2 / (N^3 - N)]$$

Where D is the difference between the ranks of X and Y and N is the no of pairs of rank observations.

4.2.5.2.4.3 Properties of the Coefficient of Correlation

There are some key properties of the coefficient of correlation. They are:

1) The value of the coefficient of correlation ranges from -1 to +1
2) A value +1.0 indicates that two variables are perfectly positively correlated
3) A value -1.0 indicates that two variables are perfectly negatively correlated
4) A value 0 indicates that there is no correlation between the two variables
5) A value greater the +0.75 implies the two variables are highly positively correlated
6) A value between +0.5 and +0.75 implies a moderate positive correlation between the two variables
7) A value less than +0.5 implies a weak positive correlation between the two variables

4.2.5.2.5 Regression

A regression is a statistical test that seeks to determine the cause and effect relationship between variables. The linear relationship that fits the two variables is called the regression line. Given that the regression studies the impact of one variable on the other it is a very useful tool for forecasting.

4.2.5.2.5.1 Coefficient of Determination

The coefficient of determination also referred to as the R-squared (R^2) indicates how close the data are to the regression line that has been fitted. In other words it is a measure of the goodness of fit. It is the square of the correlation coefficient R. The R^2 explains how much of the variation in the model is being accounted for. It varies between 0 and 1. An R^2 of 0.5 implies that 50% of the variation in the model has been accounted for. The R^2 is only an estimate of strength of the relationship between the variables and must be used in conjunction with other model statistics.

4.2.5.2.5.2 Factors Affecting Regressions

There are several factors that affect the accuracy of a regression. These include lack of normality in residuals, heteroskedasticity, multi-collinearity and auto correlation.

4.2.5.2.5.2.1 Lack of Normality in Residuals

A residual also called the error term is defined as the difference between the observed value and the forecasted value. The error term must be normally distributed. If the error term is not normally distributed forecasting errors may occur. In the present study the residuals were not normal hence a more robust estimation was used.

4.2.5.2.5.2.2 Heteroskedasticity

Heteroskedasticity is present when there is an unequal scatter of data. This occurs when the variance of all residuals from a given population are not constant. It typically arises in data sets where there is a large range between the smallest and largest observed values. It occurs when there are a relatively large number of outliers in the data and can adversely affect a forecast.

The presence of heteroskedasticity can be checked with the Breusch-Pagan test. In the present study the Breusch-Pagan test confirmed the presence of heteroskedasticity in the data. Hence a more robust estimation was used.

4.2.5.2.5.2.3 Multi-Collinearity

Multi-Collinearity occurs when there is a significant correlation among the independent variables. If this occurs then the regression may prove inaccurate. Multi-Collinearity can be detected with variance inflation factors (VIF's). If VIF's exceed 10 then there is a multi-collinearity problem. In the present study VIF's were below 2 and hence there were no multi-collinearity issues.

4.2.5.2.5.2.4 Auto Correlation

Auto correlation presents itself predominantly in time series data but can affect the outcome of regressions also. Auto correlation occurs when successive observations within a data series are correlated with each other. The Durbin Watson statistic is used to detect auto correlation. It varies between 0 and 4. Values near 0 would indicate positive auto correlation and values near 4 would indicate negative auto correlation. In the present study the Durbin Watson statistic indicated some amount of auto correlation in the data. Hence a more robust estimation was used.

4.2.5.2.5.3 Types of Regression

There are several types of regression. They include simple linear regression, multiple regression, logistic regression and the quantile regression technique used in this study.

4.2.5.2.5.3.1 Simple Linear Regression

A simple linear regression is a linear relationship fit between one independent and one dependent variable. This is the most common type of regression used and takes the form:

Y = a + b X + e, where a and b are constants and e is the error term

The constants a and b are estimated by the least squares method

4.2.5.2.5.3.2 Multiple Regression

A multiple regression is a linear relationship fit between many independent variables and one dependent variable. In this study the multiple regression technique was used exhaustively to study the impact of key determinants on bank profitability. This takes the form:

$$y = \beta_1 + \beta_2 X_2 + \beta_3 X_3 + ... + \beta_k X_k + \varepsilon$$

Source: R-bloggers

Where β_i's are the regression coefficients and ε is the error term.

4.2.5.2.5.3.3 Logistic Regression

The logistic regression describes the relationship between one dependent binary variable and one or more independent variables, which may be nominal, ordinal, interval or ratio based. The goal of the logistic regression is to predict the probability of occurrence of an event by fitting data to an appropriate logit model.

4.2.5.2.5.3.4 Quantile Regression

A quantile regression proves very useful when outliers, skewness and heteroscedasticity are prevalent in the data. Linear regressions focus on predicting the mean of dependent variable for a given set of independent variables. However, the mean may not represent the entire distribution well particularly if there are large outliers in the data.

The quantile regression technique seeks to predict a more representative quantile or percentile of the dependent variable for a given set of independent variables. If the quantile is set at 50% then it becomes a median regression. A major advantage of the quantile regression technique is that it can be used even when a few data points are missing. This study had 13 data points missing as a few banks were not listed for the entire 10-year period of the study. The quantile regression was used to study the impact of key determinants on bank profitability and generate relevant forecasts.

4.2.5.2.6 Time Series Analysis

Time series analysis uses time based data to generate forecasts for the future. It is particularly useful in analyzing serially correlated data. To generate forecasts with time series data it is required that the data series be stationary. This implies the mean and variance of the series must be constant and should not vary with time. There are several techniques like exponential smoothing and ARIMA that can be used to generate time series based forecasts.

4.2.5.2.7 Panel Data Analysis

Panel data refers to the pooling of multiple observations of several variables over multiple time periods. The variables may be related to companies, individuals or countries. A major advantage of panel data analysis lies in the fact that it allows the researcher to control for even variables that cannot be measured such as cultural factors, business practices and regulations. Thus it accounts for individual heterogeneity.

There are some key types of models that can be used in panel regressions. These include the fixed effects model and the random effects model. A fixed effects model is relevant when each company has some unique qualities that are both unmeasurable and constant over time. In the fixed effect model the slopes for each company are the same but the intercepts for each company are allowed to vary.

In the random effects model variations across companies are assumed to be random and not related to the independent variables included in the model. Rather than estimating a separate fixed effect for each firm, an overall intercept that represents the average is estimated. This study had an unbalanced panel. Even after taking this into account the panel regression did not prove as robust as the quantile regression technique and hence panel data analysis was not used in this study.

4.2.5.2.8 Forecasting

There are several key techniques like the ones discussed in the earlier unit to generate forecasts. These include regression techniques, time series analysis and panel data analysis. Given the data used in the study suffered from heteroscedasticity, lacked normality in the residuals and also had auto correlation, a robust estimation technique was required. Hence the quantile regression technique was used.

The quantile regression technique was used to fit multivariate models for ROA and ROE as a function of key determinants. These models were used to forecast ROA and

ROE for subsequent years. There are several measures of forecast quality and forecasting errors. Those used in this study are discussed below:

4.2.5.2.8.1 Forecast Quality

A useful estimator of forecast quality used in this study is the Akaike Information Criterion (AIC). The AIC will help compare the quality of a set of models and help you chose the best one among the alternatives available. Thus it serves as a basis for model selection. However it does not indicate anything about the absolute quality of the model.

4.2.5.2.8.2 Forecasting Errors

Forecasting errors indicate how accurate a forecast actually is. The two measures of forecast errors used in this study are the Mean Absolute Error (MAE) and Root Mean Squared error (RMSE). The MAE measures the average magnitude of errors in forecasts, without taking into account their direction. The RMSE on the other hand measures the average squared differences between forecasted and actual values. The lower the MAE and RMSE the better the forecast.

4.2.5.3 Hypothesis Testing

A set of 14 hypotheses were tested in the study. The level of significance which is the probability of rejecting a null hypothesis by the test when it is actually true was set at 5%. The distribution used was the normal distribution. A two tailed test which examined both sides of the data range as per the normal distribution chosen was used in testing the hypotheses. Correlation and descriptive statistics were used in hypothesis testing. The results of the hypotheses tested formed the basis for further detailed analysis.

4.3 Findings Suggestions and Conclusion

Following the analysis of the data findings were presented on the relationships between select determinants of profitability and the profitability measures chosen. Logical inferences were drawn from these findings and implications for key stake holders of the banks such as bank managers, investors and the RBI are discussed. Finally the study was concluded with a summary of its key accomplishments.

4.4 Bibliography

This study used the American Psychological Association (APA) style of referencing for all its bibliography.

The APA style uses the following format for citing journal articles:

Author, A. (Publication Year). Article title. Periodical Title, Volume (Issue), pp.-pp.

e.g., Ayadi, N., & Boujelbene, Y. (2012). The Determinants of the Profitability of the Tunisian Deposit Banks. IBIMA Business Review Journal, 1–21.

The APA style uses the following format for citing books:

Author, A. (Year of Publication). Title of work. Publisher City, State: Publisher.

e.g., Kothari, C. and Garg, G. (2014). Research methodology Methods and Techniques. 3rd ed. New Delhi: New Age International (P) Ltd.

The APA style uses the following format for citing websites:

Author, A. (Year, Month Date of Publication). Article title. Retrieved from URL

e.g., Damodaran, A. (2018). Statistical Distributions. Retrieved from http://people.stern.nyu.edu/adamodar/New_Home_Page/StatFile/statdistns.html

CHAPTER 5

ANALYSIS OF DATA

CHAPTER V

ANALYSIS OF DATA

The data relevant to this research drawn from the financial statements of banks covered 40 listed banks in India. This includes 24 public sector banks and 16 private sector banks, which have been listed for at least a 5 year period between 2006 and 2015. Analysis of the collected data was performed with descriptive statistics, correlation analysis and multiple regression analysis using the *SPSS 18.0* package and the *Gretl* econometrics package.

Firstly, the variables were subjected a test for normality to ascertain if they fit a normal distribution. Then descriptive statistics is performed on the variables to arrive at meaningful comparisons between public and private sector banks. Next, a series of hypotheses have been tested with relevant statistical tests to find the relationship between independent and dependent variables. Variables that show a strong relationship with each other were further subjected to multiple regression analysis to identify influential independent variables. Next tests are performed to check for heteroskedasticity and normality of residuals. Then a more robust regression technique such as the quantile regression was used to generate models to forecast ROA and ROE from the identified determinants.

This chapter is divided into key sub sections. The first sub section analyzes normality of the data. The second subsection examines key indicators of bank performance through descriptive statistics. The third, fourth, and fifth sub sections summarize the testing of hypotheses related to the key objectives of the study with scatter plots, correlation and regression analysis. The sixth sub section relates to the summary of the analysis. The seventh sub section focuses on developing of models with multiple regression analysis and forecasting profitability form determinants.

5.1 Test for Normality

Q-Q plots were obtained on each of the variables to ascertain if the variables followed a normal distribution. The details are summarized in Figure 5.1 to Figure 5.9:

Figure 5.1: QQ plot of the Return on Assets (ROA)

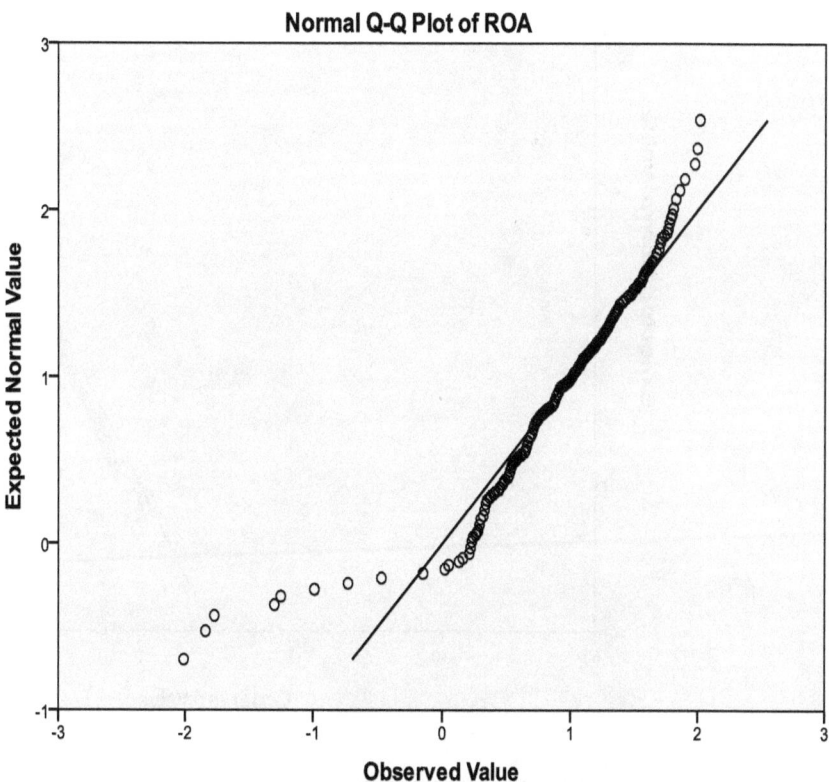

The Q-Q plot of profitability as measured by the return on assets, suggests that it follows a normal distribution

Figure 5.2: QQ plot of the Return on Equity (ROE)

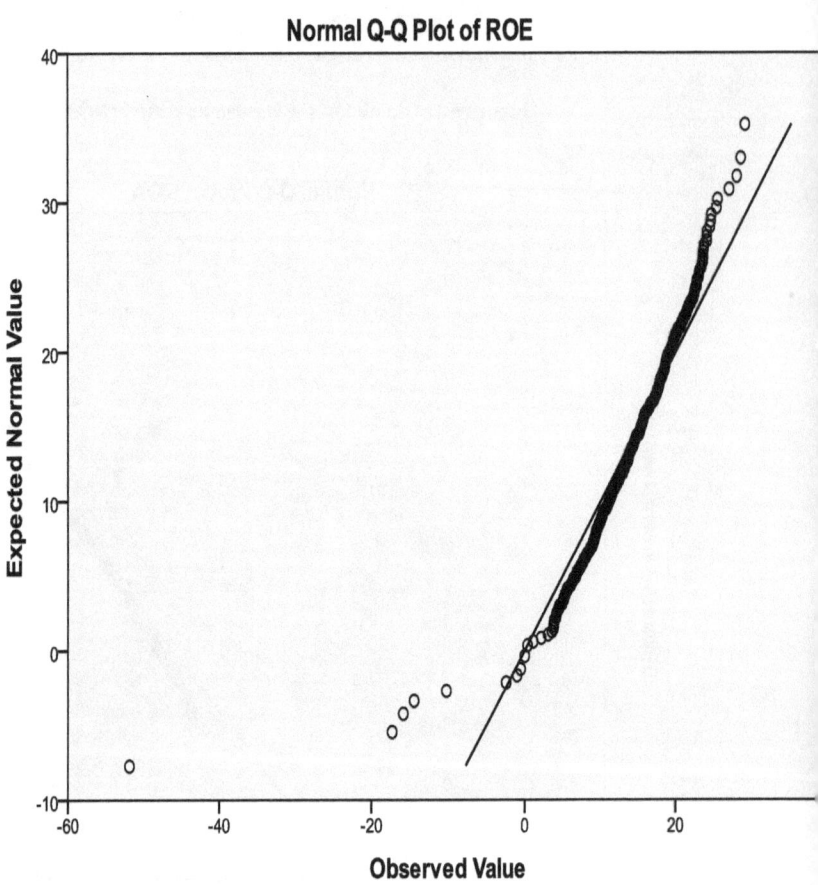

The Q-Q plot of profitability as measured by the return on equity, suggests that it follows a normal distribution

Figure 5.3: QQ plot of Bank Size

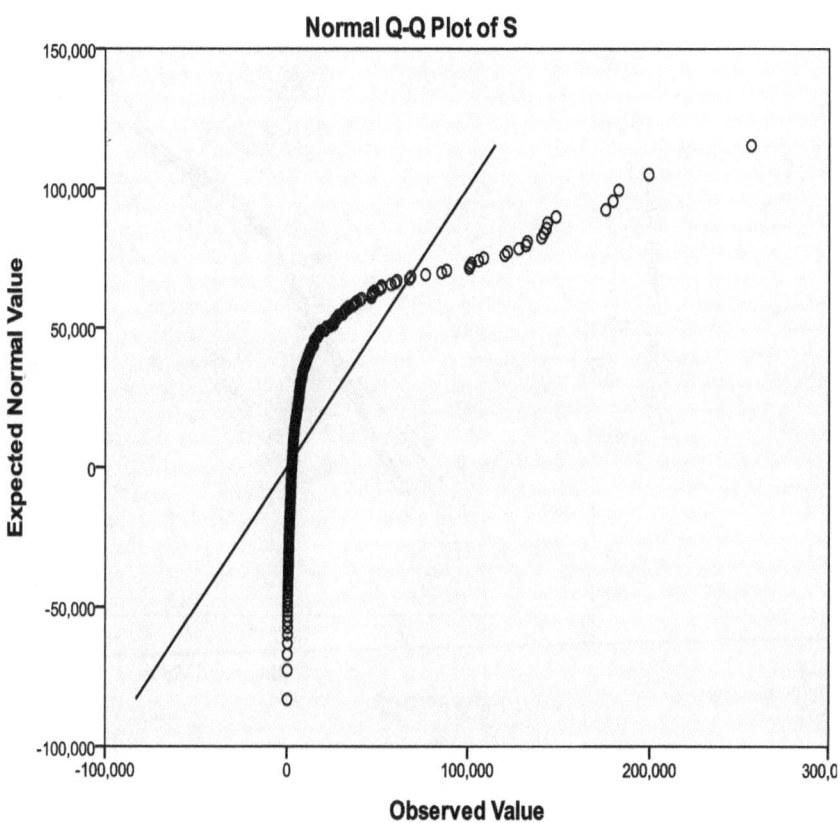

The Q-Q plot of bank size as measured by stock market capitalization, suggests that it deviates from a normal distribution

Figure 5.4: QQ plot of the Capital Adequacy Ratio

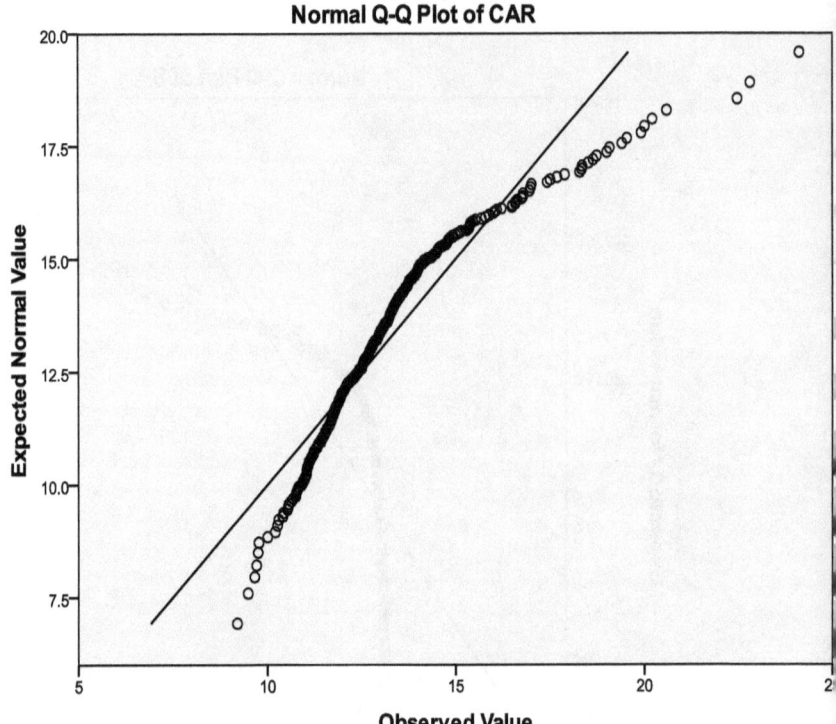

The Q-Q plot of capital adequacy as measured by the capital adequacy ratio, suggests that it follows a normal distribution

Figure 5.5: QQ plot of Business per Employee

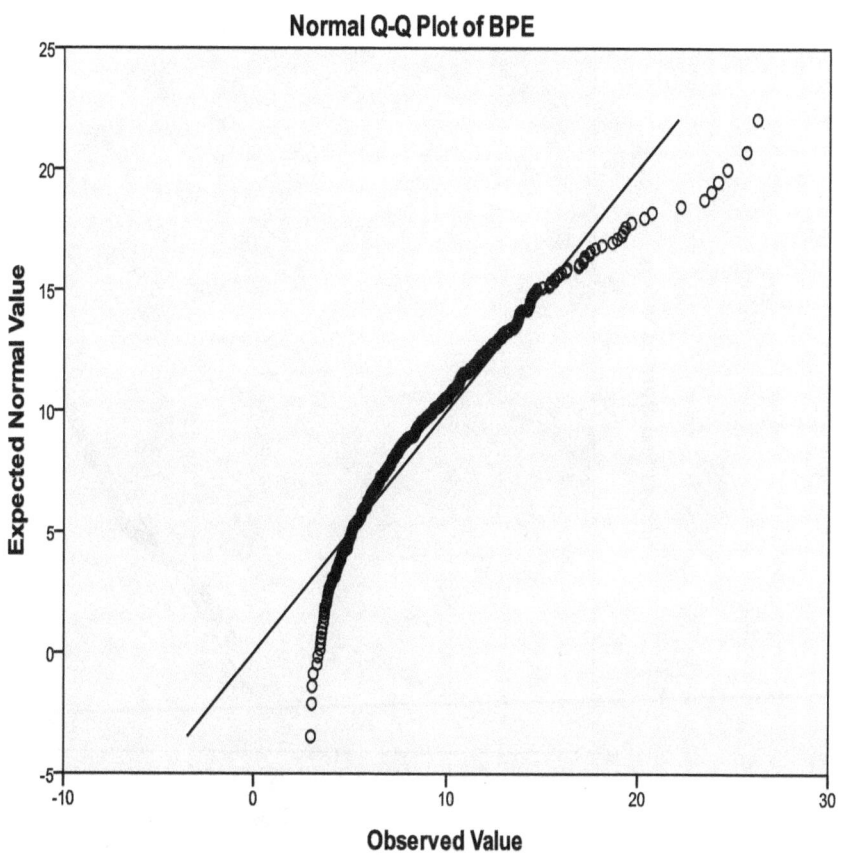

The Q-Q plot of productivity as measured by the business per employee, suggests that it follows a normal distribution

Figure 5.6: QQ plot of the Deposit Credit Ratio

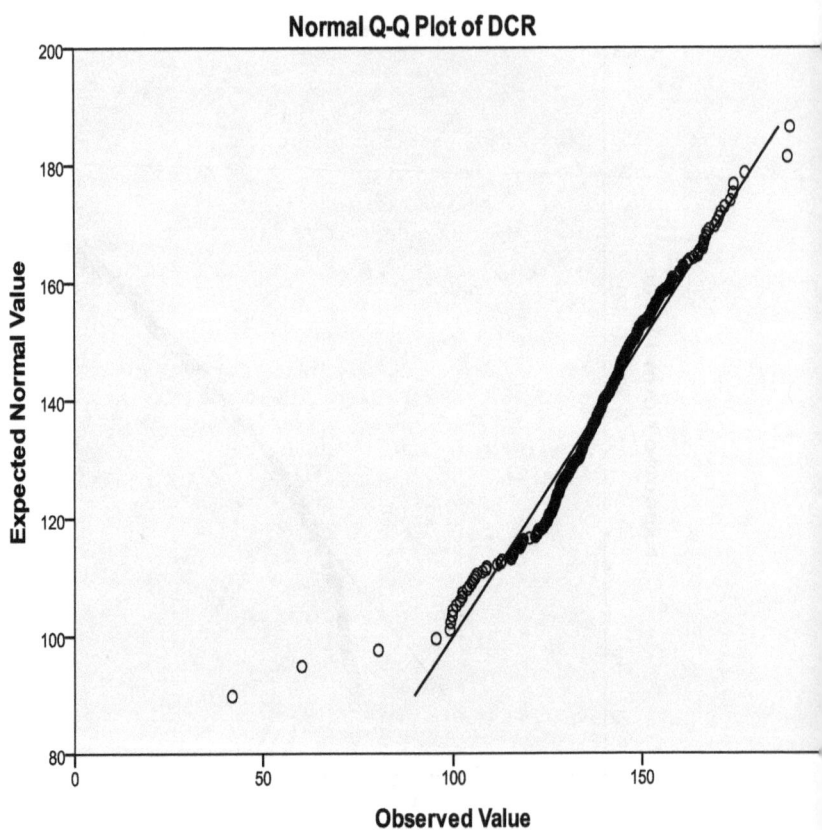

The Q-Q plot of lending activity as measured by the deposit credit ratio, suggests that it follows a normal distribution

Figure 5.7: QQ plot of Percentage Net NPA

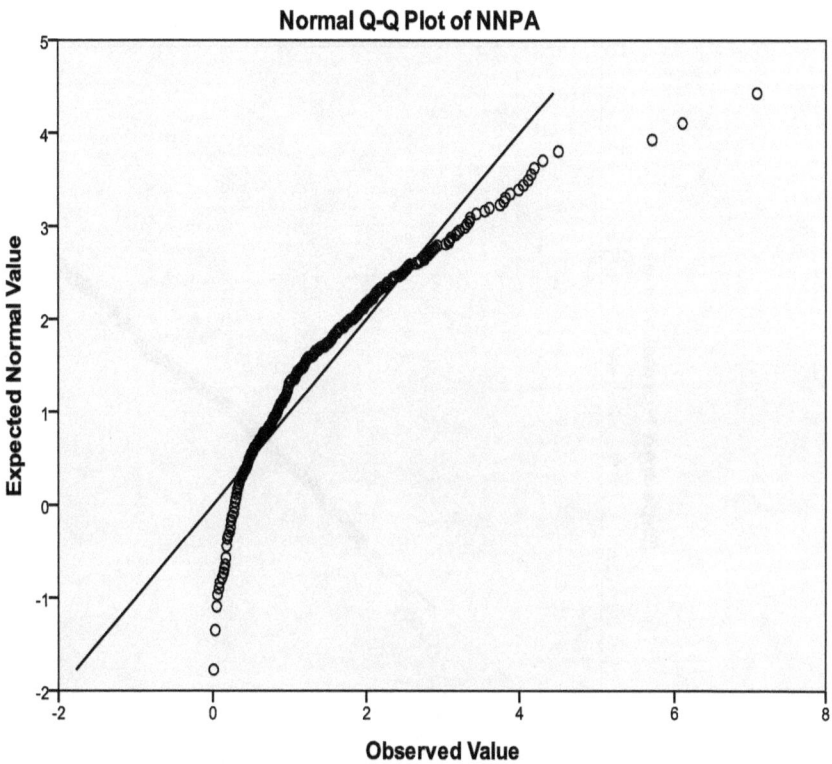

The Q-Q plot of asset quality as measured by the percentage Net NPA, suggests that it follows a normal distribution.

Figure 5.8: QQ plot of Interest Income to Average Working Funds

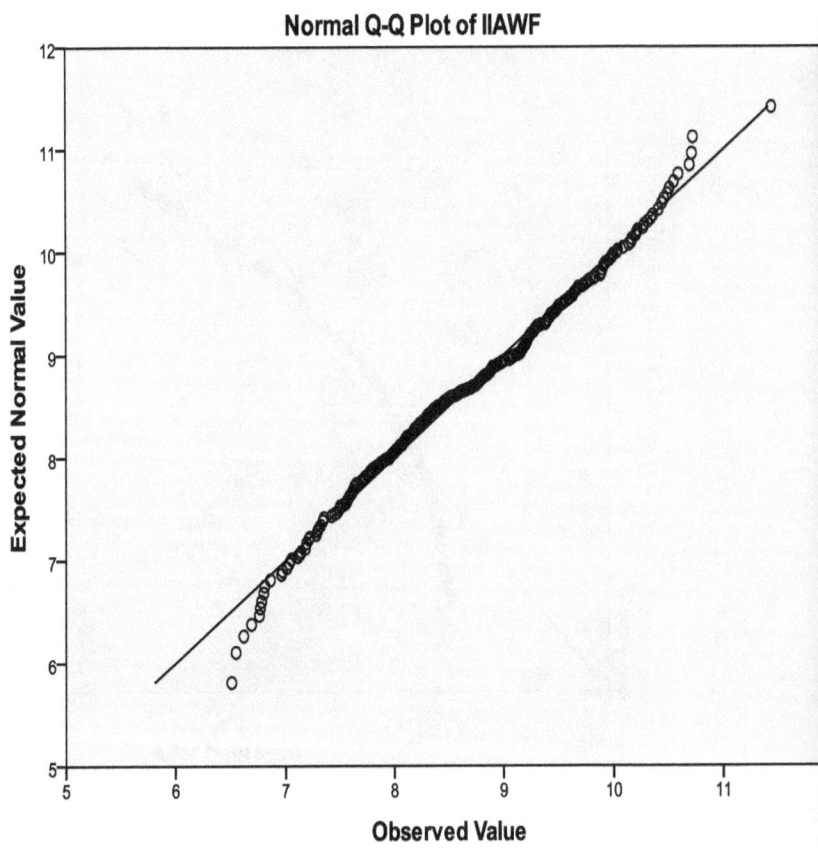

The Q-Q plot of income as measured by interest income to average working funds, suggests that it follows a normal distribution.

Figure 5.9: QQ plot of Noninterest Income to Average Working Funds

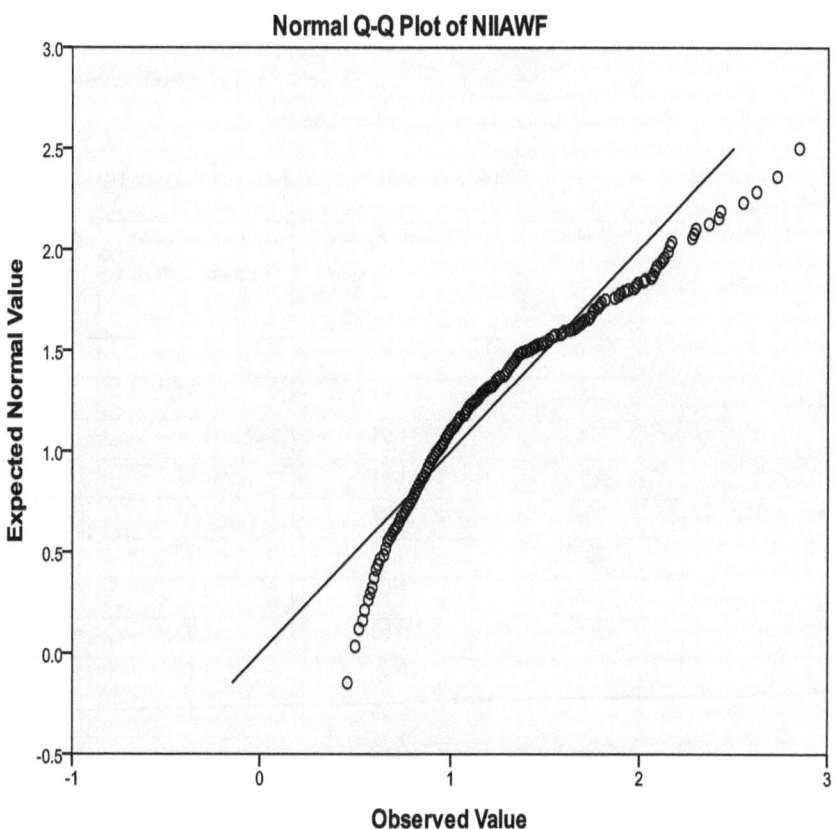

The Q-Q plot of income as measured by noninterest income to average working funds, suggests that it follows a normal distribution.

5.2 Analysis of Key Indicators of Bank Performance

The first objective of the study seeks to compare the performance of public and private sector banks. The key indicators of bank performance used in this study as variables were compared over time for public and private sector banks with descriptive statistics and the results are summarized below:

Table 5.1 Analysis of the Return on Assets (ROA)

Year	Public Sector Banks - Mean ROA (%)	Private Sector Banks - Mean ROA (%)	All Banks - Mean ROA (%)
2006	0.88	0.75	0.82
2007	0.97	0.92	0.95
2008	1.01	1.07	1.03
2009	1.01	1.01	1.01
2010	0.98	1.03	1.00
2011	0.97	1.22	1.07
2012	1.24	0.84	1.00
2013	0.82	1.33	1.02
2014	0.45	1.17	0.74
2015	0.38	1.16	0.68
Overall	0.82	1.09	0.93

Table 5.1 shows the analysis of profitability as determined by the return on assets. Private sector banks were more profitable than their public counterparts and their profitability also exceeded sector averages. This is primarily due to the fact that private sector banks have improved and maintained their asset quality over time when compared to their public counterparts.

Table 5.2 Analysis of the Return on Equity (ROE)

Year	Public Sector Banks - Mean ROE (%)	Private Sector Banks - Mean ROE (%)	All Banks - Mean ROE (%)
2006	16.40	8.83	13.15
2007	18.71	13.14	16.45
2008	20.38	14.39	17.86
2009	20.85	14.37	18.12
2010	21.46	13.63	18.32
2011	19.43	14.92	17.63
2012	15.83	15.76	15.80
2013	13.27	16.00	14.37
2014	7.54	14.60	10.36
2015	7.32	13.68	9.76
Overall	16.01	13.97	15.18

Table 5.2 shows the analysis of profitability as determined by the return on equity. The ROE of private sector banks was consistent during the study period. However, the ROE of public sector banks witnessed a gradual decline. Private sector banks were less profitable than their public counterparts and their profitability also fell below sector averages. This is because private sector banks regularly access the capital market through

equity issuances and consequently face dilution of their equity base while public sector banks are largely dependent on the government for cash infusions.

Table 5.3 Analysis of the Bank Size (S)

Year	Public Sector Banks - Mean Size (Rs. Crores)	Private Sector Banks - Mean Size (Rs. Crores)	All Banks - Mean Size (Rs. Crores)
2006	7272.34	7036.55	7171.29
2007	6660.84	10036.36	8029.30
2008	9864.94	13052.09	11206.90
2009	6583.24	7155.67	6824.27
2010	13164.13	19031.07	15510.90
2011	18612.00	23768.50	20674.60
2012	14842.47	23121.68	18154.16
2013	13777.67	28339.88	19602.56
2014	13267.90	33471.86	21349.48
2015	16849.00	52922.50	30723.42
Overall	12287.66	21764.23	16132.16

Table 5.3 shows the analysis of bank size as determined by stock market capitalization. Private sector banks were significantly larger than public sector banks and their sizes also exceeded sector averages. Hence private sector banks have created much more shareholder value over time when compared to public sector banks.

Table 5.4 Capital Adequacy Ratio (CAR)

Year	Public Sector Banks - Mean CAR (%)	Private Sector Banks - Mean CAR (%)	All Banks - Mean CAR (%)
2006	12.16	11.85	12.02
2007	12.22	12.15	12.19
2008	12.08	13.58	12.71
2009	13.66	14.70	14.10
2010	13.58	15.90	14.51
2011	13.33	14.81	13.92
2012	12.98	14.61	13.63
2013	12.18	14.72	13.20
2014	11.85	14.76	13.02
2015	11.77	14.31	12.75
Overall	12.59	14.16	13.23

Table 5.4 shows the trend of capital adequacy ratios of public and private sector banks. Private sector banks were found to be adequately capitalized when compared to their

public counterparts and their capital adequacy ratios exceeded sector averages. This is primarily due to the fact that private sector banks have improved their asset quality and accessed the capital market more frequently than their public counterparts.

Table 5.5 Analysis of Business per Employee (BPE)

Year	Public Sector Banks - Mean BPE (Rs. Crores)	Private Sector Banks - Mean BPE (Rs. Crores)	All Banks - Mean BPE (Rs. Crores)
2006	4.47	5.36	4.85
2007	5.15	5.84	5.43
2008	6.45	6.35	6.41
2009	7.89	6.66	7.37
2010	9.15	7.48	8.48
2011	10.86	8.75	10.02
2012	12.11	8.69	10.74
2013	13.52	9.44	11.89
2014	14.35	9.48	12.40
2015	15.08	10.29	13.23
Overall	10.09	7.85	9.18

Table 5.5 shows the productivity trends as determined by the business per employee. Public sector banks were found to have higher business per employee values than their private counterparts. This is probably due to the improved technological infrastructure,

training provided to public sector bank employees and the greater trust enjoyed by public sector banks when compared to their private sector competitors.

Table 5.6 Analysis of the Deposit Credit Ratio (DCR)

Year	Public Sector Banks - Mean DCR (%)	Private Sector Banks - Mean DCR (%)	All Banks - Mean DCR (%)
2006	153.53	151.68	152.74
2007	144.01	145.65	144.67
2008	139.95	142.52	141.03
2009	139.06	141.60	140.13
2010	140.63	139.21	140.06
2011	137.88	136.09	137.16
2012	133.59	131.60	132.79
2013	132.10	130.20	131.34
2014	133.15	129.83	131.82
2015	134.46	128.61	132.21
Overall	138.52	137.62	138.16

Table 5.6 shows the analysis of lending activity as determined by the deposit credit ratio. The deposit credit ratios of both public and private sector banks show a declining trend. The deposit credit ratios of both private and public sector banks were similar and in line with sector averages over the years.

Table 5.7 Analysis of Percentage Net NPA (NNPA)

Year	Public Sector Banks - Mean NNPA (%)	Private Sector Banks - Mean NNPA (%)	All Banks - Mean NNPA (%)
2006	1.17	1.54	1.33
2007	0.95	1.18	1.04
2008	0.81	0.88	0.84
2009	0.74	1.21	0.94
2010	0.99	1.10	1.03
2011	1.00	0.53	0.81
2012	1.49	0.57	1.12
2013	2.02	0.83	1.54
2014	2.77	1.05	2.09
2015	3.23	1.22	2.46
Overall	1.54	1.01	1.32

Table 5.7 shows the analysis of asset quality as determined by the percentage net NPA. Public sector banks exhibit a rapidly increasing trend in their NPAs while NPAs have been much more stable for private sector banks. Private sector banks had significantly better asset quality than their public counterparts and their asset quality also exceeded sector averages. This is due to the fact that private sector banks have been judicious in avoiding

lending to problem segments in the economy which public sector banks have been unable to avoid.

Table 5.8 Interest Income to Average Working Funds (IIAWF)

Year	Public Sector Banks - Mean IIAWF (%)	Private Sector Banks - Mean IIAWF (%)	All Banks - Mean IIAWF (%)
2006	7.31	7.61	7.44
2007	7.65	8.01	7.80
2008	8.13	8.63	8.34
2009	8.54	9.27	8.84
2010	7.88	8.53	8.14
2011	8.14	8.46	8.27
2012	9.04	9.60	9.26
2013	9.11	9.92	9.43
2014	8.79	9.80	9.19
2015	8.73	9.71	9.11
Overall	8.35	8.96	8.60

Table 5.8 reveals the profitability trends as shown by the ratio of interest income to average working funds. Private sector banks had better interest income generation than their public counterparts and their interest income generation also exceeded sector averages. This is because private sector banks have optimized their lending while

improving and maintaining their asset quality whereas public sector banks suffered setbacks from a higher proportion of stressed assets.

Table 5.9 Noninterest Income to Average Working Funds (NIIAWF)

Year	Public Sector Banks - Mean NIIAWF (%)	Private Sector Banks - Mean NIIAWF (%)	All Banks - Mean NIIAWF (%)
2006	1.15	1.42	1.27
2007	1.01	1.40	1.17
2008	1.16	1.59	1.34
2009	1.22	1.66	1.40
2010	1.12	1.64	1.33
2011	0.91	1.39	1.10
2012	0.84	1.34	1.04
2013	0.83	1.36	1.04
2014	0.83	1.38	1.05
2015	0.87	1.47	1.10
Overall	0.99	1.46	1.18

Table 5.9 indicates the trend in the other key income component of banks, the noninterest income to average working funds. Private sector banks had much better noninterest income generation than their public counterparts and their noninterest income generation also exceeded sector averages. This is because private sector banks have diversified their

income sources without compromising their asset quality when compared to public sector banks.

Thus private sector banks have higher return on assets, better asset quality, higher capital adequacy and more income generation capabilities when compared to public sector banks. Private banks also created more value for their shareholder than their public counterparts. Public and private sector banks had similar lending activities. Public sector banks had a higher return on equity and productivity when compared to private sector banks.

5.3 Impact of Bank Size, Lending Measures and Income Measures on Bank Profitability

The second objective of the study looked at the impact of bank size, lending measures and income measures on bank profitability. A series of working hypotheses were tested with the help of scatter plots, correlation analysis and univariate quantile regression analysis.

5.3.1 Impact of Bank Size on the Return on Assets (ROA)

The size of the bank can impact its profitability as measured by the ROA. The following working hypotheses were tested to examine this relationship:

Hypothesis 1:

H_0 – Bank profitability as measured by ROA is not impacted by bank size

H_1 – Bank profitability as measured by ROA is impacted by bank size

Figure 5.10 Scatter Plot of ROA versus Bank Size

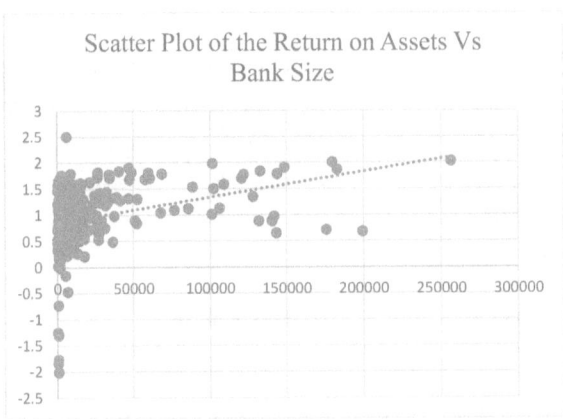

Figure 5.10 shows a scatter plot of profitability as measured by the return on assets versus bank size. The scatter plot indicated that there was a direct relationship between profitability as measured by the return on assets and bank size.

Table 5.10 Correlation Analysis between ROA and Bank Size

Dependent Variable (Profitability)	Independent Variable (Performance Indicator)	Correlation Coefficient (R)	Relationship	P Value (95% Confidence)
ROA	Bank Size	0.300	+	0.000

Table 5.10 shows the results of correlation analysis between the dependent variable ROA and the independent variable bank size. ROA showed a weak positive correlation to bank size and the correlation was statistically significant at the 95% confidence level. Thus bank profitability as measured by the return on assets was related to bank size.

Table 5.11 Results of Quantile Regression: Return on Assets as a Function of Bank Size

Dependent Variable	Independent Variable	Coefficient	P Value	AIC
ROA	Constant	0.862847	0.0000	574.9687
	Bank Size	6.22986e-06	0.0000	

Note: AIC = Akaike Information Criterion

Table 5.11 shows the results of the univariate quantile regression analysis performed with profitability as measured by the return on assets as the dependent variable and bank size as the independent variable. The results indicated a strong positive impact of bank size on the return on assets that was statistically significant at the 95% confidence level.

The results taken together suggested that there was a significant positive impact of the bank size on bank profitability as measured by the return on assets. Thus the alternate hypothesis was accepted and the null hypothesis was rejected.

5.3.2 Impact of Bank Size on the Return on Equity (ROE)

Profitability as measured by the ROE and bank size were paired to check if bank size influences the ROE. The hypotheses framed in this connection are as follows:

Hypothesis 2:

H_0 – Profitability as measured by ROE is not impacted by bank size

H_1 – Profitability as measured by ROE is impacted by bank size

Figure 5.11 Scatter Plot of ROE versus Bank Size

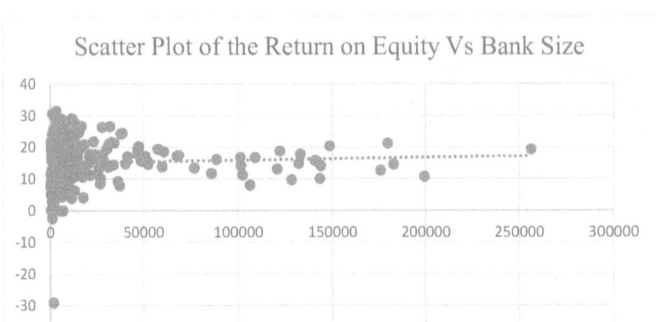

Figure 5.11 shows a scatter plot of profitability as measured by the return on equity versus bank size. The scatter plot indicated that there was a direct relationship between profitability as measured by the return on equity and bank size.

Table 5.12 Correlation Analysis between ROE and Bank Size

Dependent Variable (Share Holders Returns)	Independent Variable (Performance Indicator)	Correlation Coefficient (R)	Relationship	P Value (95% Confidence)
ROE	Bank Size	0.038	+	0.460

Table 5.12 shows the results of correlation analysis between the dependent variable ROE and the independent variable bank size. ROE showed a mild positive correlation to bank size however, the correlation was not statistically significant at the 95% confidence level. Hence profitability as measured by the return on equity was not associated with bank size.

Table 5.13 Results of Quantile Regression: Return on Equity as a Function of Bank Size

Dependent Variable	Independent Variable	Coefficient	P Value	AIC
ROE	Constant	16.1081	0.0000	2646.064
	Bank Size	−4.78264e-06	0.7578	

Note: AIC = Akaike Information Criterion

Table 5.13 shows the results of the univariate quantile regression analysis performed with profitability as measured by the return on equity as the dependent variable and bank size as the independent variable. The results indicated a weak impact of bank size on the return on equity that is not statistically significant at the 95% confidence level.

The results taken together suggested that there was no significant impact of the bank size on profitability as measured by the return on equity. Thus the alternate hypothesis was rejected and the null hypothesis was accepted in this instance.

Thus bank size significantly and positively impacted profitability as measured by the return on assets but did not impact the return on equity. Dietrich and Wanzenried, (2011) similarly found that stock market capitalization had a positive impact on bank profitability while studying 453 banks in Switzerland from 1999 to 2008.

5.3.3 Impact of Lending Measures as Indicated by the Deposit Credit Ratio on the Return on Assets (ROA) of Banks

The major income generation of banks stem from their lending activity. A key measure of this activity is the deposit credit ratio. Its impact on ROA was examined by testing the following hypotheses:

Hypothesis 3:

H_0 – Bank profitability as measured by ROA is not impacted by the deposit to credit ratio

H_1 – Bank profitability as measured by ROA is impacted by the deposit to credit ratio

Figure 5.12 Scatter Plot of ROA versus the Deposit Credit Ratio

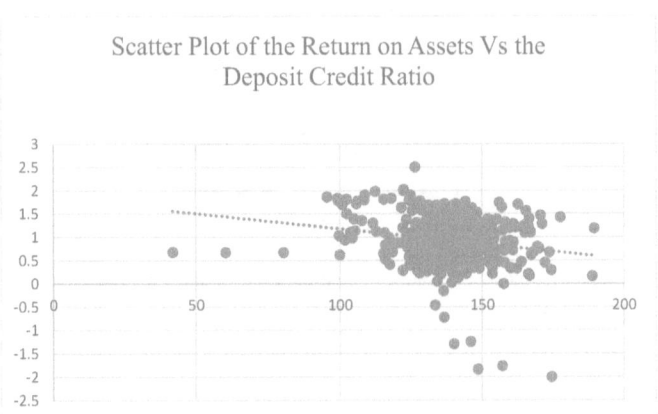

Figure 5.12 shows a scatter plot of profitability as measured by the return on assets versus the deposit credit ratio. The scatter plot indicated that there was an inverse relationship between profitability as measured by the return on assets and the deposit credit ratio.

Table 5.14 Correlation Analysis between ROA and the Deposit Credit Ratio

Dependent Variable (Profitability)	Independent Variable (Performance Indicator)	Correlation Coefficient (R)	Relationship	P Value (95% Confidence)
ROA	Deposit Credit Ratio	0.196	-	0.000

Table 5.14 shows the results of correlation analysis between the dependent variable ROA and the independent variable the deposit credit ratio. ROA showed a weak negative correlation to the deposit credit ratio and the correlation was statistically

significant at the 95% confidence level. Hence bank profitability as measured by the return on assets was related to the deposit credit ratio.

Table 5.15 Results of Quantile Regression: Return on Assets as a Function of the Deposit Credit Ratio

Dependent Variable	Independent Variable	Coefficient	P Value	AIC
ROA	Constant	1.58472	0.0000	609.1323
	Deposit Credit Ratio	−0.00469204	0.0208	

Note: AIC = Akaike Information Criterion

Table 5.15 shows the results of the univariate quantile regression analysis performed with profitability as measured by the return on assets as the dependent variable and the deposit credit ratio as the independent variable. The results indicated a negative impact of the deposit credit ratio on the return on assets that is statistically significant at the 95% confidence level.

The results taken together suggested that there was a negative impact of the deposit credit ratio on bank profitability as measured by the return on assets. Thus the alternate hypothesis was accepted and the null hypothesis was rejected.

5.3.4 Impact of Lending Measures as Indicated by the Deposit Credit Ratio on the Return on Equity (ROE) of Banks

The issue of lending activity of banks and the profitability was tested in the study. Lending, being the primary function of banks, has a direct impact on profitability. Therefore, the following working hypotheses were framed to examine the relationship between lending activity and the ROE:

Hypothesis 4:

H₀ – Bank profitability as measured by ROE is not impacted by the deposit to credit ratio

H₁ – Bank profitability as measured by ROE is impacted by the deposit to credit ratio

Figure 5.13 Scatter Plot of ROE versus the Deposit Credit Ratio

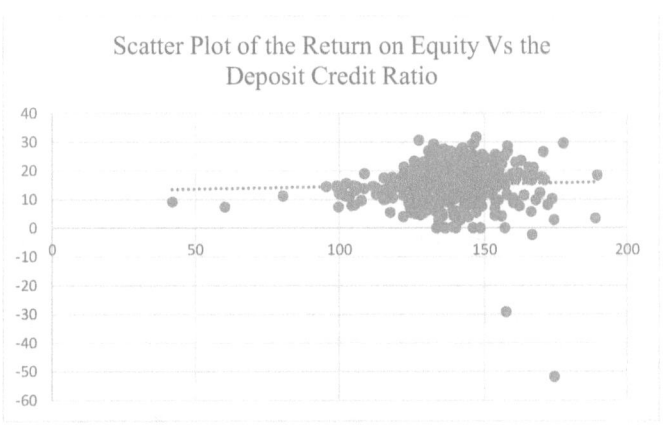

Figure 5.13 shows a scatter plot of profitability as measured by the return on equity versus the deposit credit ratio. The scatter plot indicated that there was a direct relationship between profitability as measured by the return on equity and the deposit credit ratio.

Table 5.16 Correlation Analysis between ROE and the Deposit Credit Ratio

Dependent Variable (Profitability)	Independent Variable (Performance Indicator)	Correlation Coefficient (R)	Relationship	P Value (95% Confidence)
ROE	Deposit Credit Ratio	0.036	+	0.475

Table 5.16 shows the results of correlation analysis between the dependent variable ROE and the independent variable the deposit credit ratio. ROE showed a slight positive correlation to the deposit credit ratio however the correlation was not statistically significant at the 95% confidence level. Hence profitability as measured by ROE was not related to the deposit credit ratio.

Table 5.17 Results of Quantile Regression: Return on Equity as a Function of the Deposit Credit Ratio

Dependent Variable	Independent Variable	Coefficient	P Value	AIC
ROE	Constant	5.75745	0.0641	2623.378
	Deposit Credit Ratio	0.0743206	0.0009	

Note: AIC = Akaike Information Criterion

Table 5.17 shows the results of the univariate quantile regression analysis performed with profitability as measured by the return on equity as the dependent variable and the deposit credit ratio as the independent variable. The results indicated a positive impact of the deposit credit ratio on the return on equity that is statistically significant at the 95% confidence level.

The results taken together suggested that there was a positive impact of the deposit credit ratio on bank profitability as measured by the return on equity. Thus the alternate hypothesis was accepted and the null hypothesis was rejected. Therefore, it is concluded that the deposit credit ratio negatively impacted profitability as measured by the return on assets.But it has positively impacted profitability as measured by the return on equity. In a study on 6 public sector banks from 2001 to 2010, Dhanabhakyam and Kavitha, (2012) similarly found the credit deposit ratio to be an important determinant of bank profitability.

5.3.5 Impact of Income Measures on the Return on Assets (ROA)

The key sources of income of a bank are interest and noninterest income. The impact of these key measures on bank profitability as measured by the return on assets was examined by using correlation and regression.

5.3.5.1 Impact of Interest Income to Average Working Funds on the Return on Assets (ROA)

The measure of interest income studied was interest income to average working funds. It indicates how well the banks are earning on the funds deployed. Its effect on ROA was tested through the following working hypotheses:

Hypothesis 5:

H_0 – Bank profitability as measured by ROA is not impacted by interest income to average working funds

H_1 – Bank profitability as measured by ROA is impacted by interest income to average working funds

Figure 5.14 Scatter Plot of ROA versus Interest Income to Average Working Funds

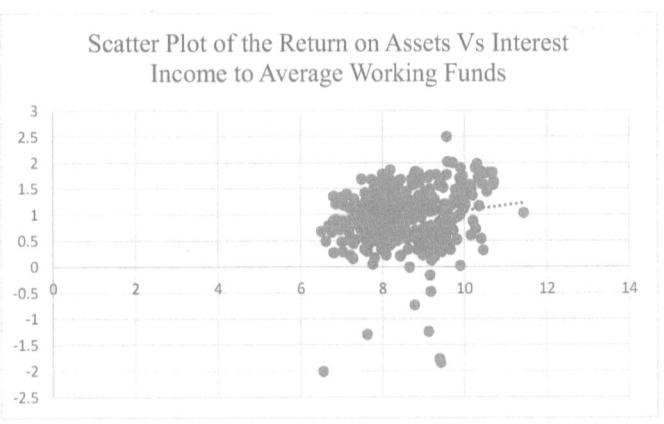

Figure 5.14 shows a scatter plot of profitability as measured by the return on assets versus interest income to average working funds. The scatter plot indicated that there was a direct relationship between profitability as measured by the return on assets and interest income to average working funds.

Table 5.18 Correlation Analysis between ROA and Interest Income to Average Working Funds

Dependent Variable (Profitability)	Independent Variable (Performance Indicator)	Correlation Coefficient (R)	Relationship	P Value (95% Confidence)
ROA	Interest Income to average Working funds	0.179	+	0.000

Table 5.18 shows the results of correlation analysis between the dependent variable ROA and the independent variable interest income to average working funds. ROA showed a weak positive correlation to interest income to average working funds and the correlation was statistically significant at the 95% confidence level. Hence bank profitability as measured by ROA was found to be related to the ratio of interest income to average working funds.

Table 5.19 Results of Quantile Regression: Return on Assets as a Function of Interest Income to Average Working Funds

Dependent Variable	Independent Variable	Coefficient	P Value	AIC
ROA	Constant	0.0379470	0.8811	600.2352
	Interest Income to Average Working Funds	0.109272	0.0002	

Note: AIC = Akaike Information Criterion

Table 5.19 shows the results of the univariate quantile regression analysis performed with profitability as measured by the return on assets as the dependent variable and interest income to average working funds as the independent variable. The results indicated a positive impact of interest income to average working funds on the return on assets that was statistically significant at the 95% confidence level.

The results taken together suggested that there was a positive impact of interest income to average working funds on bank profitability as measured by the return on assets. Thus the alternate hypothesis was accepted and the null hypothesis was rejected.

5.3.5.2 Impact of Noninterest Income to Average Working Funds on the Return on Assets (ROA)

The key noninterest income measure studied was noninterest income to average working funds. The following working hypotheses were tested to examine the impact of noninterest income to average working funds on ROA:

Hypothesis 6:

H_0 – Bank profitability as measured by ROA is not impacted by noninterest income to average working funds

H_1 – Bank profitability as measured by ROA is impacted by noninterest income to average working funds

Figure 5.15 Scatter Plot of ROA versus Noninterest Income to Average Working Funds

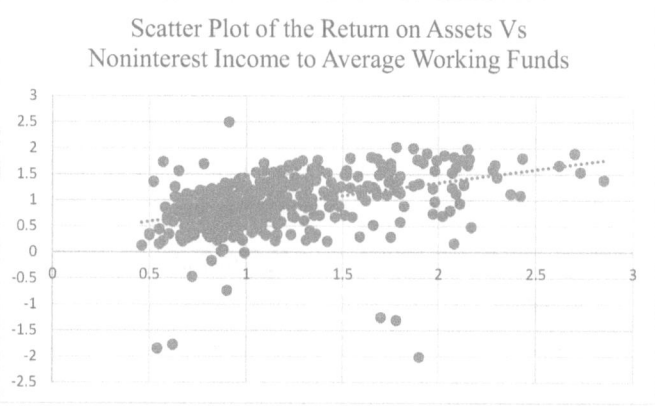

Figure 5.15 shows a scatter plot of profitability as measured by the return on assets versus noninterest income to average working funds. The scatter plot indicated that there was a direct relationship between profitability as measured by the return on assets and noninterest income to average working funds.

Table 5.20 Correlation Analysis between ROA and Noninterest Income to Average Working Funds

Dependent Variable (Profitability)	Independent Variable (Performance Indicator)	Correlation Coefficient (R)	Relationship	P Value (95% Confidence)
ROA	Noninterest Income to average Working Funds	0.412	+	0.000

Table 5.20 shows the results of correlation analysis between the dependent variable ROA and the independent variable noninterest income to average working funds. ROA showed a weak positive correlation to noninterest income to average working funds and the correlation was statistically significant at the 95% confidence level. Hence bank profitability as measured by ROA was related to noninterest income to average working funds.

Table 5.21 Results of Quantile Regression: Return on Assets as a Function of Noninterest Income to Average Working Funds

Dependent Variable	Independent Variable	Coefficient	P Value	AIC
ROA	Constant	0.259677	0.0000	483.0189
	Noninterest Income to Average Working Funds	0.607527	0.0000	

Note: AIC = Akaike Information Criterion

Table 5.21 shows the results of the univariate quantile regression analysis performed with profitability as measured by the return on assets as the dependent variable and noninterest income to average working funds as the independent variable. The results indicated a strong positive impact of noninterest income to average working funds on the return on assets that was statistically significant at the 95% confidence level.

The results taken together suggested that there was a strong positive impact of noninterest income to average working funds on bank profitability as measured by the return on assets. Thus the alternate hypothesis was accepted and the null hypothesis was rejected.

5.3.6 Impact of Income Measures as Indicated on the Return on Equity (ROE)

The impact of the above income measures on the return on equity was assessed below.

5.3.6.1 Impact of Interest Income to Average Working Funds on the Return on Equity (ROE)

Similar to the earlier analysis of ROA, the income measures have been related with the ROE in this section of the study. ROE represents the return on shareholders' funds which is the overall return to the sharehoders. In the current context the income measure, both interest and non interest measures, have been correlated with the ROE.

The impact of interest income on ROE was ascertained by testing the following working hypotheses:

Hypothesis 7:

H_0 – Profitability as measured by ROE is not impacted by interest income to average working funds

H_1 – Profitability as measured by ROE is impacted by interest income to average working funds

Figure 5.16 Scatter Plot of ROE versus Interest Income to Average Working Funds

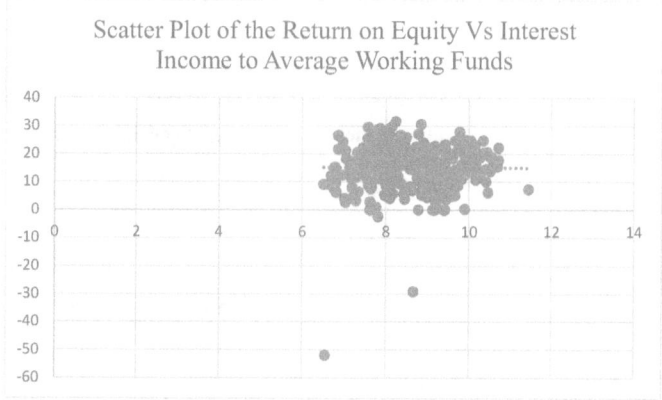

Figure 5.16 shows a scatter plot of profitability as measured by the return on equity versus interest income to average working funds. The scatter plot indicated that there was a direct relationship between profitability as measured by the return on equity and interest income to average working funds.

Table 5.22 Correlation Analysis between ROE and Interest Income to Average Working Funds

Dependent Variable (Profitability)	Independent Variable (Performance Indicator)	Correlation Coefficient (R)	Relationship	P Value (95% Confidence)
ROE	Interest Income to average Working Funds	0.005	-	0.928

Table 5.22 shows the results of correlation analysis between the dependent variable ROE and the independent variable interest income to average working funds. ROE showed a slight negative correlation to interest income to average working funds but the correlation was not statistically significant at the 95% confidence level. Hence profitability as measured by the return on equity was not related to interest income to average working funds.

Table 5.23 Results of Quantile Regression: Return on Equity as a Function of Interest Income to Average Working Funds

Dependent Variable	Independent Variable	Coefficient	P Value	AIC
ROE	Constant	22.0802	0.0000	2644.052
	Interest Income to Average Working Funds	−0.713755	0.1795	

Note: AIC = Akaike Information Criterion

Table 5.23 shows the results of the univariate quantile regression analysis performed with profitability as measured by the return on equity as the dependent variable and interest income to average working funds as the independent variable. The results indicated a negative impact of interest income to average working funds on the return on equity that was not statistically significant at the 95% confidence level.

The results taken together suggested that interest income to average working funds did not impact bank profitability as measured by the return on equity. Thus the alternate hypothesis was rejected and the null hypothesis was accepted.

5.3.6.2 Impact of Noninterest Income to Average Working Funds on the Return on Equity (ROE)

The impact of noninterest income on ROE was assessed by testing the following working hypotheses:

Hypothesis 8:

H_0 – Bank profitability as measured by ROE is not impacted by noninterest income to average working funds

H_1 – Bank profitability as measured by ROE is impacted by noninterest income to average working funds

Figure 5.17 Scatter Plot of ROE versus Noninterest Income to Average Working Funds

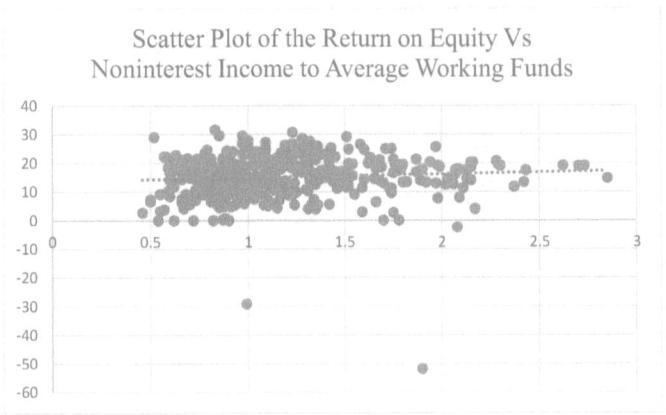

Figure 5.17 shows a scatter plot of profitability as measured by the return on equity versus noninterest income to average working funds. The scatter plot indicated that there was a direct relationship between profitability as measured by the return on equity and noninterest income to average working funds.

Table 5.24 Correlation Analysis between ROE and Noninterest Income to Average Working Funds

Dependent Variable (Share Holders Returns)	Independent Variable (Performance Indicator)	Correlation Coefficient (R)	Relationship	P Value (95% Confidence)
ROE	Noninterest Income to average Working Funds	0.074	+	0.147

Table 5.24 shows the results of correlation analysis between the dependent variable ROE and the independent variable noninterest income to average working funds. ROE showed a slight positive correlation to noninterest income to average working funds however the correlation was not statistically significant at the 95% confidence level. Hence profitability as measured by the return on equity was not related to noninterest income to average working funds.

Table 5.25 Results of Quantile Regression: Return on Equity as a Function of Noninterest Income to Average Working Funds

Dependent Variable	Independent Variable	Coefficient	P Value	AIC
ROE	Constant	13.0560	0.0000	2635.333
	Noninterest Income to Average Working Funds	2.20000	0.0201	

Note: AIC = Akaike Information Criterion

Table 5.25 shows the results of the univariate quantile regression analysis performed with profitability as measured by the return on equity as the dependent variable and noninterest income to average working funds as the independent variable. The results indicated a positive impact of noninterest income to average working funds on the return on equity that was statistically significant at the 95% confidence level.

The results taken together suggest that noninterest income to average working funds impacted bank profitability as measured by the return on equity positively. Thus the alternate hypothesis was accepted and the null hypothesis was rejected.

Thus interest income to average working funds impacted bank profitability as measured by the return on assets positively but did not impact profitability as measured by the return on equity. Interest income is the predominant source of income for most banks. Ganesan, (2001) also observed that interest income was a very important determinant of profitability of a large sample of public sector banks in India studied over a 4 year period.

Noninterest income to average working funds positively impacted bank profitability as measured by both the return on assets and the return on equity. Fee based income can provide a very good diversification to bank income streams and is probably a reason why private banks in India are more profitable than their public counterparts. Sufian, (2009) similarly observed for a sample of Malaysian banks between 2000 and 2004, that banks that derive a higher proportion of their income from noninterest sources were much more profitable. Bodla and Verma, (2006) also found that noninterest income was a significant determinant of profitability of a sample of 27 public sector banks in India studied between 1991 and 2004.

5.4 Impact of Employee Productivity on Bank Profitability

The third objective of the study was to specifically look at the impact of the productivity of the banks workforce on bank profitability. A series of working hypotheses were tested with the help of scatter plots, correlation analysis and univariate quantile regression analysis.

5.4.1 Impact of Employee Productivity as Measured by Business per Employee on the Return on Assets (ROA)

The productivity of bank employees was studied using business per employee. Its impact on ROA was measured by testing the following working hypotheses:

Hypothesis 9:

H_0 – Bank profitability as measured by ROA is not impacted by business per employee

H_1 – Bank profitability as measured by ROA is impacted by business per employee

Figure 5.18 Scatter Plot of ROA versus Business per Employee

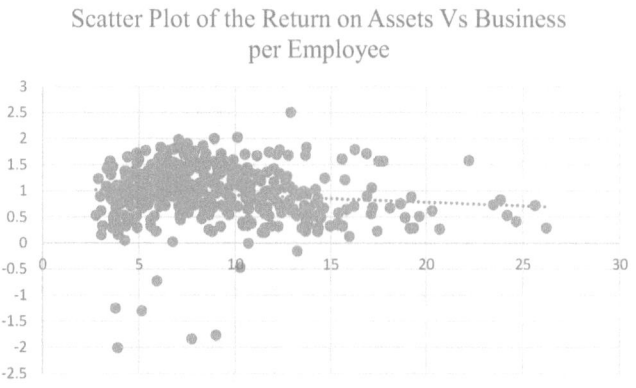

Figure 5.18 shows a scatter plot of profitability as measured by the return on assets versus the business per employee. The scatter plot indicates that there was an inverse relationship between profitability as measured by the return on assets and the business per employee.

Table 5.26 Correlation Analysis between ROA and Business per Employee

Dependent Variable (Profitability)	Independent Variable (Performance Indicator)	Correlation Coefficient (R)	Relationship	P Value (95% Confidence)
ROA	Business per Employee	0.110	-	0.030

Table 5.26 shows the results of correlation analysis between the dependent variable ROA and the independent variable business per employee. ROA showed a small negative correlation to business per employee and the correlation was statistically significant at the 95% confidence level. Hence bank profitability as measured by the return on assets was related to the business per employee.

Table 5.27 Results of Quantile Regression: Return on Assets as a Function of Business per Employee

Dependent Variable	Independent Variable	Coefficient	P Value	AIC
ROA	Constant	1.21324	0.0000	590.2632
	Business per Employee	−0.0294906	0.0002	

Note: AIC = Akaike Information Criterion

Table 5.27 shows the results of the univariate quantile regression analysis performed with profitability as measured by the return on assets as the dependent variable and the business per employee as the independent variable. The results indicate a negative impact of the business per employee on the return on assets that was statistically significant at the 95% confidence level.

The results taken together suggest that there was a negative impact of the business per employee on bank profitability as measured by the return on assets. Thus the alternate hypothesis was accepted and the null hypothesis was rejected.

5.4.2 Impact of Employee Productivity as Measured by Business per Employee on the Return on Equity (ROE)

The impact of business per employee on the ROE was assessed by testing the following working hypotheses:

Hypothesis 10:

H_0 – Bank profitability as measured by ROE is not impacted by business per employee

H_1 – Bank profitability as measured by ROE is impacted by business per employee

Figure 5.19 Scatter Plot of ROE versus Business per Employee

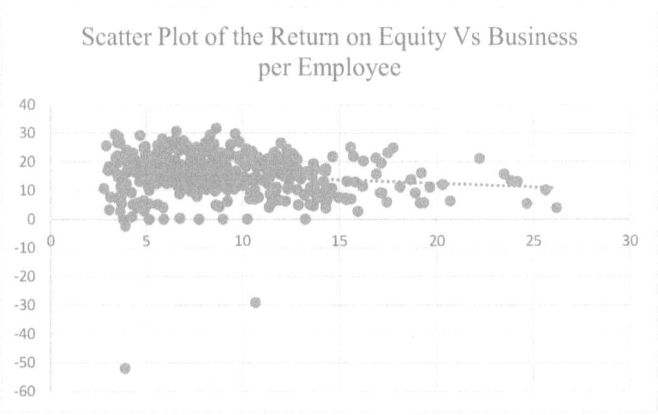

Figure 5.19 shows a scatter plot of profitability as measured by the return on equity versus the business per employee. The scatter plot indicated that there was an inverse relationship between profitability as measured by the return on equity and the business per employee.

Table 5.28 Correlation Analysis between ROE and Business per Employee

Dependent Variable (Share Holders Returns)	Independent Variable (Performance Indicator)	Correlation Coefficient (R)	Relationship	P Value (95% Confidence)
ROE	Business per Employee	0.140	-	0.006

Table 5.28 shows the results of correlation analysis between the dependent variable ROE and the independent variable business per employee. ROE showed a small negative correlation to business per employee and the correlation was statistically significant at the 95% confidence level. Hence bank profitability as measured by the return on equity was related to the business per employee.

Table 5.29 Results of Quantile Regression: Return on Equity as a Function of Business per Employee

Dependent Variable	Independent Variable	Coefficient	P Value	AIC
ROE	Constant	18.9114	0.0000	2621.531
	Business per Employee	−0.375683	0.0000	

Note: AIC = Akaike Information Criterion

Table 5.29 shows the results of the univariate quantile regression analysis performed with profitability as measured by the return on equity as the dependent variable and the business per employee as the independent variable. The results indicated a negative impact of the business per employee on the return on equity that was statistically significant at the 95% confidence level.

The results taken together suggest that there is a negative impact of the business per employee on bank profitability as measured by the return on equity. Thus the alternate hypothesis is accepted and the null hypothesis is rejected.

Thus the business per employee negatively impacted profitability as measured by the return on assets and return on equity. While this may sound counter intuitive a very high productivity of the work force may result in aggressive lending and ultimately lower asset quality which in turn could result in lower return on assets and return on equity. This has been observed in the case of public sector banks which have had a higher productivity than their private counterparts.

5.5 Impact of Capital Adequacy and Asset Quality on Bank Profitability

The fourth objective of the study was to examine the impact of capital adequacy and asset quality on bank profitability. A series of working hypotheses were tested with the help of scatter plots, correlation analysis and univariate quantile regression analysis.

5.5.1 Impact of Capital adequacy as measured by the Capital Adequacy Ratio on the Return on Assets (ROA)

Given the implementation of *Basel III* norms for the Indian banking sector, capital adequacy has become a very important metric for banks. Capital adequacy is assessed via the capital adequacy ratio and its impact on ROA is examined by testing the following working hypotheses:

Hypothesis 11:

H_0 – Bank profitability as measured by ROA is not impacted by the capital adequacy ratio

H_1– Bank profitability as measured by ROA is impacted by the capital adequacy ratio

Figure 5.20 Scatter Plot of ROA versus the Capital Adequacy Ratio

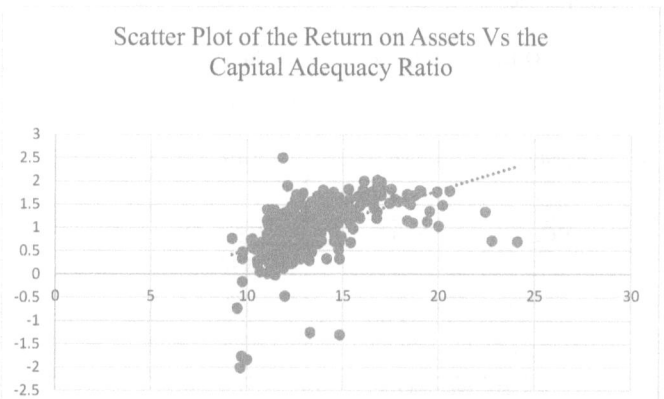

Figure 5.20 shows a scatter plot of profitability as measured by the return on assets versus the capital adequacy ratio. The scatter plot indicated that there was a direct relationship between profitability as measured by the return on assets and the capital adequacy ratio.

Table 5.30 Correlation Analysis between ROA and the Capital Adequacy Ratio

Dependent Variable (Profitability)	Independent Variable (Performance Indicator)	Correlation Coefficient (R)	Relationship	P Value (95% Confidence)
ROA	Capital Adequacy Ratio	0.499	+	0.000

Table 5.30 shows the results of correlation analysis between the dependent variable ROA and the independent variable the capital adequacy ratio. ROA showed a positive correlation to the capital adequacy ratio and the correlation was statistically significant at the 95% confidence level. Hence bank profitability as measured by ROA was related to the capital adequacy ratio.

Table 5.31 Results of Quantile Regression: Return on Assets as a Function of the Capital Adequacy ratio

Dependent Variable	Independent Variable	Coefficient	P Value	AIC
ROA	Constant	−0.885676	0.0000	449.8586
	Capital Adequacy Ratio	0.138514	0.0000	

Note: AIC = Akaike Information Criterion

Table 5.31 shows the results of the univariate quantile regression analysis performed with profitability as measured by the return on assets as the dependent variable and the capital adequacy ratio as the independent variable. The results indicated a strong positive impact of the capital adequacy ratio on the return on assets that was statistically significant at the 95% confidence level.

The results taken together suggested that there was a strong positive impact of the capital adequacy ratio on bank profitability as measured by the return on assets. Thus the alternate hypothesis was accepted and the null hypothesis was rejected.

5.5.2 Impact of Capital adequacy as measured by the Capital Adequacy Ratio on the Return on Equity (ROE)

To understand the impact of the capital adequacy ratio on the ROE, the following working hypotheses were tested:

Hypothesis 12:

H_0 – Bank profitability as measured by ROE is not impacted by the capital adequacy ratio

H_1 – Bank profitability as measured by ROE is impacted by the capital adequacy ratio

Figure 5.21 Scatter Plot of ROE versus the Capital Adequacy Ratio

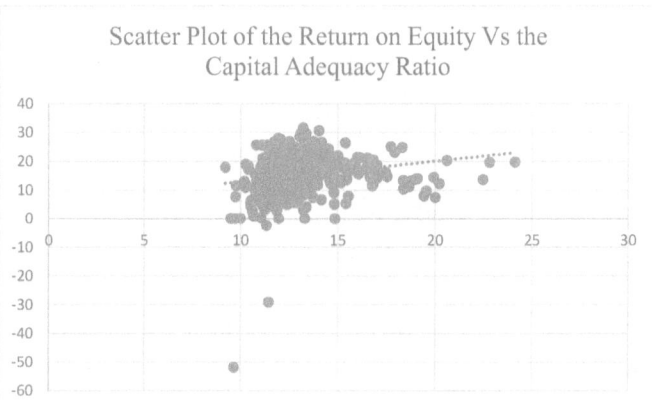

Figure 5.21 shows a scatter plot of profitability as measured by the return on equity versus the capital adequacy ratio. The scatter plot indicated that there was a direct relationship between profitability as measured by the return on equity and the capital adequacy ratio.

Table 5.32 Correlation Analysis between ROE and the Capital Adequacy Ratio

Dependent Variable (Profitability)	Independent Variable (Performance Indicator)	Correlation Coefficient (R)	Relationship	P Value (95% Confidence)
ROE	Capital Adequacy Ratio	0.200	+	0.000

Table 5.32 shows the results of correlation analysis between the dependent variable ROE and the independent variable the capital adequacy ratio. ROE showed a weak positive correlation to the capital adequacy ratio and the correlation was statistically significant at the 95% confidence level. Hence bank profitability as measured by the return on equity was related to the capital adequacy ratio.

Table 5.33 Results of Quantile Regression: Return on Equity as a Function of the Capital Adequacy ratio

Dependent Variable	Independent Variable	Coefficient	P Value	AIC
ROE	Constant	9.45112	0.0025	2635.656
	Capital Adequacy Ratio	0.470175	0.0432	

Note: AIC = Akaike Information Criterion

Table 5.33 shows the results of the univariate quantile regression analysis performed with profitability as measured by the return on equity as the dependent variable and the capital adequacy ratio as the independent variable. The results indicated a positive impact of the capital adequacy ratio on the return on equity that was statistically significant at the 95% confidence level.

The results taken together suggested that there was a positive impact of the capital adequacy ratio on bank profitability as measured by the return on equity. Thus the alternate hypothesis was accepted and the null hypothesis was rejected.

The capital adequacy ratio positively impacted bank profitability as measured by both the return on assets and the return on equity. With *Basel III* requirements being implemented by the RBI in a phased manner for the banking sector in India capital adequacy requirements have come to the forefront and it is hence a very important determinant of profitability.

In examining the profitability of a sample of Indonesian banks from 1990-2005 Sufian & Habibullah, (2010) also found that highly capitalized banks were more profitable. In studying the profitability of banks in 12 Islamic countries Masood and Ashraf, (2012) similarly observed that banks having higher capital adequacy levels were more profitable than banks with lower capital adequacy levels.

5.5.3 Impact of Asset Quality as Measured by the Percentage Net NPA on the Return on Assets (ROA)

Asset quality issues have dominated the Indian banking sector in the last five years as nonperforming assets have more than doubled. Asset quality can be assessed by monitoring the percentage net NPA. The following working hypotheses were tested to determine the effect of the percentage net NPA on ROA:

Hypothesis 13:

H_0 – Bank profitability as measured by ROA is not impacted by the percentage Net NPA

H_1 – Bank profitability as measured by ROA is impacted by the percentage Net NPA

Figure 5.22 Scatter Plot of ROA versus Percentage Net NPA

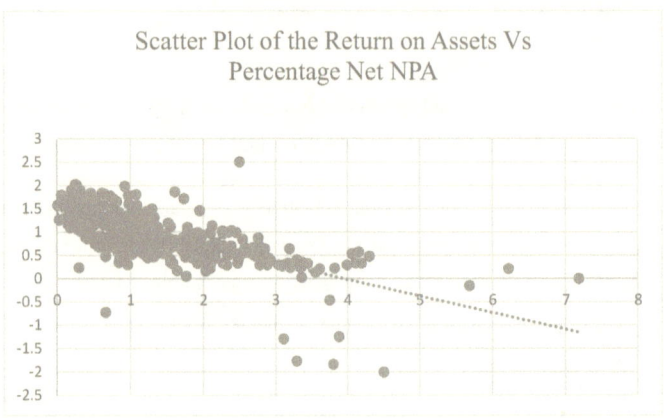

Figure 5.22 shows a scatter plot of profitability as measured by the return on assets versus the percentage Net NPA. The scatter plot indicates that there was an inverse relationship between profitability as measured by the return on assets and the percentage Net NPA.

Table 5.34 Correlation Analysis between ROA and Percentage Net NPA

Dependent Variable (Profitability)	Independent Variable (Performance Indicator)	Correlation Coefficient (R)	Relationship	P Value (95% Confidence)
ROA	Percentage Net NPA	0.683	-	0.000

Table 5.34 shows the results of correlation analysis between the dependent variable ROA and the independent variable percentage Net NPA. ROA showed a strong negative correlation to percentage Net NPA and the correlation was statistically significant at the 95% confidence level. Hence bank profitability as measured by the return on assets was related to percentage Net NPA.

Table 5.35 Results of Quantile Regression: Return on Assets as a Function of Percentage Net NPA

Dependent Variable	Independent Variable	Coefficient	P Value	AIC
ROA	Constant	1.38743	0.0000	318.3517
	Percentage Net NPA	−0.346535	0.0000	

Note: AIC = Akaike Information Criterion

Table 5.35 shows the results of the univariate quantile regression analysis performed with profitability as measured by the return on assets as the dependent variable and the percentage Net NPA as the independent variable. The AIC value was also the lowest when compared to all other independent variables, suggesting that percentage Net NPA was the most influential independent variable. The results indicated a strong negative impact of the percentage Net NPA on the return on assets that was statistically significant at the 95% confidence level.

The results taken together suggest that there was a negative impact of the percentage Net NPA on bank profitability as measured by the return on assets. Thus the alternate hypothesis was accepted and the null hypothesis was rejected.

5.5.4 Impact of Asset Quality as Measured by the Percentage Net NPA on Bank Profitability as Measured by the Return on Equity (ROE)

To assess the impact of asset quality on the ROE, the following working hypotheses were tested:

Hypothesis 14:

H_0 – Bank profitability as measured by ROE is not impacted by the percentage Net NPA

H_1 – Bank profitability as measured by ROE is impacted by the percentage Net NPA

Figure 5.23 Scatter Plot of ROE versus Percentage Net NPA

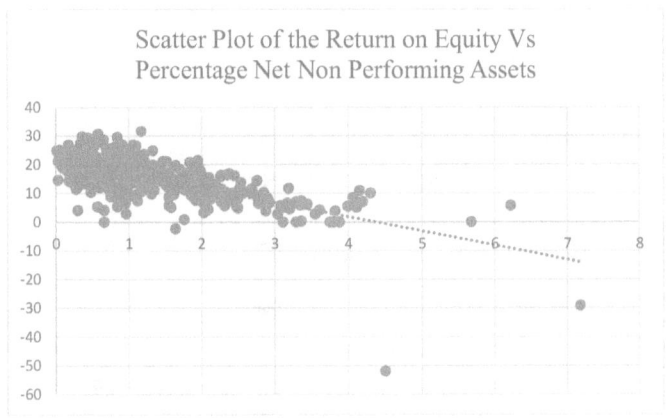

Figure 5.23 shows a scatter plot of profitability as measured by the return on equity versus the percentage Net NPA. The scatter plot indicates that there was an inverse relationship between profitability as measured by the return on equity and the percentage Net NPA.

Table 5.36 Correlation Analysis between ROE and Percentage Net NPA

Dependent Variable (Profitability)	Independent Variable (Performance Indicator)	Correlation Coefficient (R)	Relationship	P Value (95% Confidence)
ROE	Percentage Net NPA	0.677	-	0.000

Table 5.36 shows the results of correlation analysis between the dependent variable ROE and the independent variable percentage Net NPA. ROE showed a strong negative correlation to percentage Net NPA and the correlation was statistically significant at the

95% confidence level. Hence bank profitability as measured by the return on equity was related to percentage Net NPA.

Table 5.37 Results of Quantile Regression: Return on Equity as a Function of Percentage Net NPA

Dependent Variable	Independent Variable	Coefficient	P Value	AIC
ROE	Constant	21.2672	0.0000	2379.725
	Percentage Net NPA	−4.57402	0.0000	

Note: AIC = Akaike Information Criterion

Table 5.37 shows the results of the univariate quantile regression analysis performed with profitability as measured by the return on equity as the dependent variable and the percentage Net NPA as the independent variable. The results indicate a strong negative impact of the percentage Net NPA on the return on equity that was statistically significant at the 95% confidence level. The AIC value was also the lowest when compared to all other independent variables, suggesting that percentage Net NPA was the most influential independent variable.

The results taken together suggest that there was a negative impact of the percentage Net NPA on bank profitability as measured by the return on equity. Thus the alternate hypothesis was accepted and the null hypothesis was rejected.

Thus the percentage Net NPA negatively impacted profitability as measured by the return on assets and return on equity. Asset quality issues have been significantly affecting the Indian banking sector over the last five years and it is no surprise that it was the most influential determinant of profitability.

Growe et al., (2014) studied U.S. regional banks during the period from 1994 to 2011 and also found that provisions for credit losses negatively impacted bank profitability. Miller and Noulas, (1997) found that provisions for loan losses and net charge offs had a significant negative effect on the profitability of large commercial banks in the US. Similarly Zarrouk et al., (2016) found that asset quality significantly influenced profitability of a sample of 51 Islamic banks during the period between 1994 and 2012 in the Middle East and North Africa (MENA) region.

5.6 Summary of Analysis

The major observations from the analysis are summarized below:

Table 5.38: Summary of Analysis

Determinant	Measure	Profitability Measure	Impact
Percentage Net NPA	Asset Quality	Return on Assets	Negative
Percentage Net NPA	Asset Quality	Return on Equity	Negative
Capital Adequacy Ratio	Capital Adequacy	Return on Assets	Positive
Capital Adequacy Ratio	Capital Adequacy	Return on Equity	Positive
Noninterest Income to Average Working Funds	Income	Return on Assets	Positive
Noninterest Income to Average Working Funds	Income	Return on Equity	Positive
Bank Size	Size	Return on Assets	Positive
Bank Size	Size	Return on Equity	Positive
Deposit Credit Ratio	Lending	Return on Assets	Negative
Deposit Credit Ratio	Lending	Return on Equity	Positive
Interest Income to Average Working Funds	Income	Return on Assets	Positive
Interest Income to Average Working Funds	Income	Return on Equity	None
Business per Employee	Productivity	Return on Assets	Negative
Business per Employee	Productivity	Return on Equity	Negative

Table 5.38 shows the impact of the determinants studied on bank profitability. Measures of size, capital adequacy and income impacted bank profitability positively while measures of asset quality and productivity had a negative impact on bank profitability. Lending measures varied in their impact on bank profitability.

5.7 Forecasting

The final objective of the study was to develop quantitative models to forecast profitability as measured by the return on assets and return on equity from key determinants. Multiple regression analysis was used to fit appropriate models which were then used to forecast the return on assets and return on equity.

5.7.1 Model Fitting

The key determinants of ROA and ROE were used to construct multi-variate models with the goal of forecasting ROA and ROE for each of the banks for the financial years ending March 2016 and March 2017 respectively. The models were further refined by starting with the most influencing variable and adding one more variable in the order of influence monitoring the adjusted R^2 each time. This is continued until the adjusted R^2 started decreasing. The models obtained were checked for heteroskedasticity, normality in residuals, auto-correlation and multi-collinearity before final forecasts are made. If heteroskedasticity, auto correlation or multi collinearity was present then a more robust quantile regression was performed which helped to eliminate the effect of any significant outliers in the data.

5.7.1.1 Model for Profitability as Measured by the Return on Assets (ROA)

Based on the analysis performed the following model was considered for ROA:

$$ROA = A + B \times NNPA + C \times CAR + D \times NIIAWF + E \times S + F \times DCR + G \times IIAWF + H \times BPE + \varepsilon$$

Where A, B, C, D, E, F, G and H are constant coefficients to be estimated from the multivariate regression and ε is the error term.

Table 5.39 Results of Regression Analysis

Dependent Variable	Independent Variable	R^2	Adjusted R^2	P Value	F Value (ANOVA)	Durbin Watson	Variance Inflation Factor
ROA	NNPA	0.467	0.465	0.000	336.698	0.902	1.000

Table 5.39 shows the results of regression analysis between the dependent variable ROA and the independent variable the percentage Net NPA. The R^2 indicates that the model fit was reasonable. The P and F values confirmed the goodness of the fit. The Durbin Watson coefficient is less than 1.0 and implied that some amount of auto correlation was present.

Table 5.40 Results of Bi-Variate Regression Analysis

Dependent Variable	Independent Variables	R^2	Adjusted R^2	P Value	F Value (ANOVA)	Durbin Watson	Variance Inflation Factor
ROA	NNPA	0.543	0.541	0.000	228.175	0.976	1.141
	CAR						1.141

Table 5.40 shows the results of bi-variate regression analysis between the dependent variable ROA and the independent variables the percentage Net NPA and the capital adequacy ratio. The increasing adjusted R^2 indicated that the model fit had improved. The P and F values confirmed the goodness of the fit. The Durbin Watson coefficient is less than 1.0 and implied that some amount of auto correlation was present. The variance inflation factors are less than 5 and indicated the absence of multi-collinearity among the independent variables.

Table 5.41 Results of Multi-Variate Regression Analysis

Dependent Variable	Independent Variables	R^2	Adjusted R^2	P Value	F Value (ANOVA)	Durbin Watson	Variance Inflation Factor
ROA	NNPA	0.557	0.554	0.000	160.665	0.929	1.208
	CAR						1.247
	NIIAWF						1.231

Table 5.41 shows the results of multi-variate regression analysis between the dependent variable ROA and the independent variables the percentage Net NPA, the capital adequacy ratio and noninterest income to average working funds. The increasing adjusted R^2 indicated that the model fit had improved. The P and F values confirmed the goodness of the fit. The Durbin Watson coefficient is less than 1.0 and implied that some amount of auto correlation was present. The variance inflation factors are less than 5 and indicated the absence of multi-collinearity among the independent variables.

Table 5.42 Results of Multi-Variate Regression Analysis

Dependent Variable	Independent Variables	R^2	Adjusted R^2	P Value	F Value (ANOVA)	Durbin Watson	Variance Inflation Factor
ROA	NNPA	0.575	0.570	0.000	129.154	0.955	1.224
	CAR						1.333
	NIIAWF						1.348
	S						1.239

Table 5.42 shows the results of multi-variate regression analysis between the dependent variable ROA and the independent variables the percentage Net NPA, the capital adequacy ratio, noninterest income to average working funds and bank size. The increasing adjusted R^2 indicated that the model fit had improved. The P and F values confirmed the goodness of the fit. The Durbin Watson coefficient is less than 1.0 and implied that some amount of auto correlation was present. The variance inflation factors are less than 5 and indicated the absence of multi-collinearity among the independent variables.

Table 5.43 Results of Multi-Variate Regression Analysis

Dependent Variable	Independent Variables	R^2	Adjusted R^2	P Value	F Value (ANOVA)	Durbin Watson	Variance Inflation Factor
ROA	NNPA	0.577	0.571	0.000	103.891	0.952	1.245
	CAR						1.413
	NIIAWF						1.361
	S						1.326
	DCR						1.257

Table 5.43 shows the results of multi-variate regression analysis between the dependent variable ROA and the independent variables the percentage Net NPA, the capital adequacy ratio, noninterest income to average working funds, bank size and the deposit

credit ratio. The increasing adjusted R^2 indicated that the model fit had improved. The P and F values confirmed the goodness of the fit. The Durbin Watson coefficient is less than 1.0 and implied that some amount of auto correlation was present. The variance inflation factors are less than 5 and indicated the absence of multi-collinearity among the independent variables.

Table 5.44 Results of Multi-Variate Regression Analysis

Dependent Variable	Independent Variables	R^2	Adjusted R^2	P Value	F Value (ANOVA)	Durbin Watson	Variance Inflation Factor
ROA	NNPA	0.607	0.601	0.000	97.993	0.984	1.259
	CAR						1.499
	NIIAWF						1.362
	S						1.415
	DCR						1.342
	IIAWF						1.185

Table 5.44 shows the results of multi-variate regression analysis between the dependent variable ROA and the independent variables the percentage Net NPA, the capital adequacy ratio, noninterest income to average working funds, bank size, the deposit credit ratio and interest income to average working funds. The increasing adjusted R^2 indicated that the model fit had improved. The P and F values confirmed the goodness of the fit. The Durbin Watson coefficient is less than 1.0 and implied that some amount of auto

correlation was present. The variance inflation factors are less than 5 and indicated the absence of multi-collinearity among the independent variables.

Table 5.45 Results of Multi-Variate Regression Analysis

Dependent Variable	Independent Variables	R^2	Adjusted R^2	P Value	F Value (ANOVA)	Durbin Watson	Variance Inflation Factor
ROA	NNPA	0.608	0.601	0.000	83.938	0.985	1.292
	CAR						1.499
	NIIAWF						1.459
	S						1.415
	DCR						1.535
	IIAWF						1.206
	BPE						1.347

Table 5.45 shows the results of multi-variate regression analysis between the dependent variable ROA and the independent variables the percentage Net NPA, the capital adequacy ratio, noninterest income to average working funds, bank size, the deposit credit ratio, interest income to average working funds and business per employee. The adjusted R^2 had started to decrease and indicates that the model fit is no longer improving. The P and F values confirmed the goodness of the fit. The Durbin Watson coefficient is less than 1.0 and implied that some amount of auto correlation was present. Variance inflation factors below 5.000 confirm that multi collinearity was not an issue.

Thus business per employee did not significantly impact the model and can be removed from the original model. The model for ROA now reduced to:

$$ROA = A + B \times NNPA + C \times CAR + D \times NIIAWF + E \times S + F \times DCR + G \times IIAWF + \varepsilon$$

Where A, B, C, D, E, F and G are constant coefficients to be estimated from the multivariate regression and ε is the error term. The model must now be checked for normality in its residuals and for heteroskedasticity.

Table 5.46 Tests for Normality of Residuals and Heteroskedasticity

Test	Null Hypothesis	Test Statistic	P value
Test for normality of residual	Error is normally distributed	Chi-square(2) = 156.293	0.0000
Breusch Pagan test for heteroskedasticity	Heteroskedasticity not present	LM = 208.625	0.0000

Table 5.46 shows the results of the tests for normality of residuals and heteroskedasticity. The results of both tests rejected the null hypotheses and consequently the alternate hypotheses are accepted. Thus the residuals are not normally distributed and heteroskedasticity was present.

While the residuals not being normally distributed will not have a significant impact on the forecast, auto correlation and heteroskedasticity will definitely pose challenges to model accuracy hence a more robust estimation was required. Hence the Quantile Regression technique was considered to get an unbiased and more robust estimation. The Akaike Criterion (AIC) was used to select the best model fit. Bank size was excluded from the independent variables as it was the only variable which was not a ratio and didn't follow a normal distribution and including it would have affected the accuracy of the model.

Table 5.47 Selection of Quantile

Quantile	AIC
0.25	311.1707
0.50	176.9137
0.75	193.8602

Table 5.47 shows the selection of the relevant quantile using the Akaike Criterion (AIC). The AIC is the lowest for the 0.50 quantile and it was chosen as the quantile for the robust estimation.

Table 5.48 Results of Quantile Regression: ROA as a Function of All Independent Variables

Dependent Variable	Independent Variable	Coefficient	P Value	AIC
ROA	Constant	0.0651733	0.7448	179.9969
	CAR	0.0517951	0.0000	
	BPE	−0.00326525	0.2166	
	DCR	−0.00111844	0.1196	
	NNPA	−0.275865	0.0000	
	IIAWF	0.0620946	0.0000	
	NIIAWF	0.190132	0.0000	

Table 5.48 shows the estimation of the coefficients from the quantile regression performed between the dependent variable ROA and all the independent variables. The contributing independent variables as indicated by the P Values were bank size, the capital adequacy ratio, percentage Net NPA, interest income to average working funds and noninterest income to average working funds. Other variables were excluded from further analysis.

The model for ROA can now be written as:

$$ROA = A + B \times NNPA + C \times CAR + D \times NIIAWF + E \times IIAWF + \varepsilon$$

Table 5.49 Results of Quantile Regression: ROA as a Function of Significant Independent Variables

Dependent Variable	Independent Variable	Coefficient	P Value	AIC
ROA	Constant	−0.130459	0.4249	176.9137
	CAR	0.0553797	0.0000	
	NNPA	−0.278430	0.0000	
	IIAWF	0.0582868	0.0005	
	NIIAWF	0.183913	0.0000	

Table 5.49 shows the estimation of the coefficients from the quantile regression performed between the dependent variable ROA and the contributing independent variables. The AIC value shows the model fit had improved. The coefficients and constant were determined from the quantile regression shown above.

Thus the most important determinants of ROA were the capital adequacy ratio, percentage net NPA, interest income to average working funds and noninterest income to average working funds. Percentage Net NPA impacted ROA negatively while the other variables had a positive effect on ROA.

The model for ROA can now be written as:

$$ROA = -0.130459 - 0.278430 NNPA + 0.0553797 CAR + 0.183913 NIIAWF + 0.0582868 IIAWF + \varepsilon$$

5.7.1.2 Model for Profitability as Measured by the Return on Equity (ROE)

Based on the earlier analysis performed the following model was considered for ROE:

$$ROE = A + B \times NNPA + C \times CAR + D \times BPE + \varepsilon$$

Where A, B, C and D are constant coefficients to be estimated from the multivariate regression and ε is the error term.

Table 5.50 Results of Regression Analysis

Dependent Variable	Independent Variable	R^2	Adjusted R^2	P Value	F Value (ANOVA)	Durbin Watson	Variance Inflation Factor
ROE	NNPA	0.459	0.457	0.000	326.168	0.942	1.000

Table 5.50 shows the results of regression analysis between the dependent variable ROE and the independent variable the percentage Net NPA. The R^2 indicates that the model fit was reasonably good. The P and F values confirmed the goodness of the fit. The Durbin Watson coefficient was less than 1.0 and implied that some amount of auto correlation was present. Variance inflation factors below 5.000 confirm that multi collinearity was not an issue.

Table 5.51 Results of Bi-Variate Regression Analysis

Dependent Variable	Independent Variables	R^2	Adjusted R^2	P Value	F Value (ANOVA)	Durbin Watson	Variance Inflation Factor
ROE	NNPA	0.460	0.458	0.000	163.777	0.961	1.141
	CAR						1.141

Table 5.51 shows the results of bi-variate regression analysis between the dependent variable ROE and the independent variables the percentage Net NPA and the capital

adequacy ratio. The R^2 indicates that the model fit was reasonably good. The P and F values confirmed the goodness of the fit. The Durbin Watson coefficient is less than 1.0 and implied that some amount of auto correlation was present. Variance inflation factors below 5.000 confirm that multi collinearity was not an issue.

Table 5.52 Results of Multi-Variate Regression Analysis

Dependent Variable	Independent Variables	R^2	Adjusted R^2	P Value	F Value (ANOVA)	Durbin Watson	Variance Inflation Factor
ROE	NNPA	0.462	0.457	0.000	109.459	0.963	1.226
	CAR						1.148
	BPE						1.075

Table 5.52 shows the results of multi-variate regression analysis between the dependent variable ROE and the independent variables the percentage Net NPA, the capital adequacy ratio and business per employee. The adjusted R^2 had started to decrease and indicated that the model fit had not improved further. The P and F values confirmed the goodness of the fit. The Durbin Watson coefficient is less than 1.0 and implied that some amount of auto correlation was present. Variance inflation factors below 5.000 confirm that multi collinearity was not an issue.

Thus business per employee did not significantly impact the model and can be removed from the original model. The model for ROE now reduced to:

ROE = A + B x NNPA + C x CAR

Where A, B and C are constant coefficients to be estimated from the multivariate regression and ε is the error term.

The model must now be checked for normality in its residuals and also for heteroskedasticity.

Table 5.53 Tests for Normality of Residuals and Heteroskedasticity

Test	Null Hypothesis	Test Statistic	P value
Test for normality of residual	Error is normally distributed	Chi-square(2) = 191.551	0.0000
Breusch Pagan test for heteroskedasticity	Heteroskedasticity not present	LM = 307.889	0.0000

Table 5.53 shows the results of the tests for normality of residuals and heteroskedasticity. The results of both tests rejected the null hypotheses and consequently the alternate hypotheses are accepted. Thus the residuals were not normally distributed and heteroskedasticity was present.

While the residuals not being normally distributed do not have a significant impact on forecasting, heteroskedasticity and auto correlation will definitely pose challenges to the accuracy of the model hence a more robust estimation was required. Hence the Quantile Regression technique was used to get an unbiased estimation. The Akaike Criterion (AIC) was used to fit the best model. Here bank size is excluded from the independent variables as it was the only variable which was not a ratio and didn't follow a normal distribution and including it would have affected model accuracy.

Table 5.54 Selection of Quantile

Quantile	AIC
0.25	2457.086
0.50	2359.663
0.75	2412.430

Table 5.54 shows the selection of the relevant quantile using the Akaike Criterion (AIC). The AIC is the lowest for the 0.50 quantile and it was chosen as the quantile for the robust estimation.

Table 5.55 Results of Quantile Regression: ROE as a Function of All Independent Variables

Dependent Variable	Independent Variable	Coefficient	P Value	AIC
ROE	Constant	20.2364	0.0000	2365.158
	CAR	−0.0935351	0.5173	
	BPE	−0.0126808	0.8537	
	DCR	0.0302377	0.1079	
	NNPA	−5.18141	0.0000	
	IIAWF	0.115501	0.6912	
	NIIAWF	−1.62265	0.0168	

Table 5.55 shows the estimation of the coefficients from the quantile regression performed between the dependent variable ROE and all the independent variables. The contributing independent variables as indicated by the P Values at 10% significance were percentage Net NPA, the deposit credit ratio and noninterest income to average working funds. Other variables were excluded from further analysis.

The most important determinants of ROE were the percentage net NPA, noninterest income to average working funds and the deposit-credit ratio. The deposit-credit ratio had a positive impact on ROE while the other two variables had a negative impact on ROE.

The model for ROE can now be written as:

$$ROE = A + B \times NNPA + C \times NIIAWF + D \times DCR$$

Table 5.56 Results of Quantile Regression: ROE as a Function of Significant Independent Variables

Dependent Variable	Independent Variable	Coefficient	P Value	AIC
ROE	Constant	18.8191	0.0000	2359.663
	NNPA	−5.05440	0.0000	
	NIIAWF	−1.55803	0.0020	
	DCR	0.0361263	0.0031	

Table 5.56 shows the estimation of the coefficients from the quantile regression performed between the dependent variable ROE and the contributing independent variables. The AIC value shows the model fit had improved. The coefficients and constant were determined from the quantile regression shown above.

The model for ROE can now be written as:

ROE = 18.8191−5.05440NNPA −1.55803NIIAWF + 0.0361263DCR + ε

5.7.2 Prediction of ROA and ROE

The models developed for ROA and ROE were used to generate forecasts for the financial years ending March 2016 and March 2017. The models for ROA and ROE are as follows:

ROA = −0.130459 − 0.278430NNPA + 0.0553797CAR + 0.183913NIIAWF + 0.0582868IIAWF + ε

ROE = 18.8191−5.05440NNPA −1.55803NIIAWF + 0.0361263DCR + ε

The forecasted values are shown below:

Table 5.57 Forecast for ROA for the Financial Year Ending March 2016

Bank	ROA Actual	ROA Forecasted	Forecast Parameters
Allahabad Bank	-0.31	-0.77	RMSE = 0.35617
Andhra Bank	0.26	-0.07	MAE = 0.22821
Axis Bank	1.72	1.37	
Bank of Baroda	-0.8	-0.25	
Bank of India	0.94	-1.15	
Bank of Maharashtra	0.07	-0.61	
Canara Bank	-0.52	-0.67	
Central Bank	-0.48	-0.93	
City Union Bank	1.5	1.15	
Corporation Bank	-0.23	-0.69	
DCB Bank	1.14	1.26	
Dena Bank	-1.02	-0.67	
Dhanlaxmi Bank	-1.61	0.16	
Federal Bank	0.57	0.89	
HDFC Bank	1.89	1.49	
Indian Overseas Bank	-0.97	-2.24	

ICICI Bank	1.49	0.86
IDBI Bank	-1.09	-0.70
Indian Bank	0.36	0.09
IndusInd Bank	1.91	1.71
Jammu & Kashmir Bank	0.57	0.00
Karnataka Bank	0.76	0.60
Karur Vysya Bank	1.03	1.20
Kotak Mah. Bank	1.19	1.30
Lakshmi Vilas Bank	0.69	0.94
Oriental Bank	0.07	-0.63
Punjab & Sind Bank	0.34	-0.16
Punjab National Bank	-0.61	-1.28
State Bank of Travancore	0.31	0.44
South India Bank	0.55	0.41
State Bank of Bikaner	0.83	0.49
State Bank of India	0.46	0.19
State Bank of Mysore	0.44	0.07
Syndicate Bank	-0.56	-0.11

UCO Bank	-1.25	-1.47	
Union Bank	0.35	-0.31	
United Bank	-0.22	-1.39	
Vijaya Bank	0.28	-0.13	
Yes Bank	1.78	1.60	

Table 5.57 shows the forecasted values for ROA for all banks for the financial year ending March 2016. The root mean squared error (RMSE) and the mean absolute error (MAE) confirmed variability in the forecast.

Table 5.58 Forecast for ROE for the Financial Year Ending March 2016

Bank	ROE Actual	ROE Forecasted	Forecast Parameters
Allahabad Bank	0	-11.98	RMSE = 5.5749
Andhra Bank	4.91	-1.13	MAE = 3.8389
Axis Bank	16.81	15.99	
Bank of Baroda	0	-2.58	
Bank of India	0	-16.48	
Bank of Maharashtra	1.38	-10.01	
Canara Bank	0	-9.77	
Central Bank	0	-14.29	

City Union Bank	15.47	13.68
Corporation Bank	0	-10.30
DCB Bank	11.85	17.27
Dena Bank	0	-9.11
Dhanlaxmi Bank	0	9.71
Federal Bank	6.01	14.02
HDFC Bank	18.26	19.17
Indian Overseas Bank	0	-37.60
ICICI Bank	11.62	3.55
IDBI Bank	0	-12.55
Indian Bank	5.41	1.13
IndusInd Bank	16.59	16.56
Jammu & Kashmir Bank	6.64	1.11
Karnataka Bank	11.73	10.70
Karur Vysya Bank	12.87	18.60
Kotak Mah. Bank	10.97	15.31
Lakshmi Vilas Bank	11.74	15.79
Oriental Bank	1.16	-11.17
Punjab & Sind Bank	6.8	-0.26

Punjab National Bank	0	-21.55	
State Bank of Travancore	5.75	8.37	
South India Bank	9.3	7.83	
State Bank of Bikaner	13.34	7.82	
State Bank of India	7.3	1.94	
State Bank of Mysore	7.92	0.79	
Syndicate Bank	0	-0.54	
UCO Bank	0	-22.66	
Union Bank	6.99	-4.62	
United Bank	0	-22.66	
Vijaya Bank	6.02	-1.30	
Yes Bank	19.94	18.61	

Table 5.58 shows the forecasted values for ROE for all banks for the financial year ending March 2016. The root mean squared error (RMSE) and the mean absolute error (MAE) confirmed variability in the forecast.

Table 5.59 Forecast for ROA for the Financial Year Ending March 2017

Bank	ROA Actual	ROA Forecasted	Forecast Parameters
Allahabad Bank	-0.13	-1.33	RMSE = 0.35617
Andhra Bank	0.08	-0.85	MAE = 0.22821
Axis Bank	0.65	0.91	
Bank of Baroda	0.2	-0.22	
Bank of India	-0.24	-0.84	
Bank of Maharashtra	-0.86	-2.17	
Canara Bank	0.2	-0.51	
Central Bank	-0.8	-1.72	
City Union Bank	1.5	1.09	
Corporation Bank	0.23	-1.11	
DCB Bank	0.93	1.19	
Dena Bank	0.67	-1.83	
Dhanlaxmi Bank	0.1	0.37	
Federal Bank	0.84	0.91	
HDFC Bank	1.88	1.40	
Indian Overseas Bank	-1.21	-2.75	
ICICI Bank	1.35	0.25	

IDBI Bank	-1.37	-2.59	
Indian Bank	0.67	0.04	
IndusInd Bank	1.86	1.65	
Jammu & Kashmir Bank	2.04	-0.29	
Karnataka Bank	0.74	0.61	
Karur Vysya Bank	1	0.64	
Kotak Mah. Bank	1.73	1.29	
Lakshmi Vilas Bank	0.83	0.79	
Oriental Bank	-0.46	-1.32	
Punjab & Sind Bank	0.2	-1.03	
Punjab National Bank	0.19	-1.03	
South India Bank	0.57	0.84	
State Bank of India	0.41	0.22	
Syndicate Bank	0.12	-0.26	
UCO Bank	-0.75	-1.47	
Union Bank	0.13	-0.65	
United Bank	0.16	-1.60	
Vijaya Bank	0.49	0.04	
Yes Bank	1.81	1.52	

Table 5.59 shows the forecasted values for ROA for all banks for the financial year ending March 2017. The root mean squared error (RMSE) and the mean absolute error (MAE) confirmed variability in the forecast.

Table 5.60 Forecast for ROE for the Financial Year Ending March 2017

Bank	ROE Actual	ROE Forecasted	Forecast Parameters
Allahabad Bank	0	-23.23	RMSE = 5.5749
Andhra Bank	1.67	-16.12	MAE = 3.8389
Axis Bank	6.76	8.04	
Bank of Baroda	3.44	-1.06	
Bank of India	0	-12.42	
Bank of Maharashtra	0	-37.14	
Canara Bank	3.92	-9.98	
Central Bank	0	-27.83	
City Union Bank	15.18	12.54	
Corporation Bank	4.84	-19.81	
DCB Bank	10.82	17.32	
Dena Bank	0	-31.18	
Dhanlaxmi Bank	1.89	18.82	

Federal Bank	9.76	15.51	
HDFC Bank	17.95	18.89	
Indian Overseas Bank	0	-48.74	
ICICI Bank	10.66	-9.14	
IDBI Bank	0	-44.86	
Indian Bank	10.06	0.06	
IndusInd Bank	15.26	16.56	
Jammu & Kashmir Bank	0	-1.64	
Karnataka Bank	10.76	8.87	
Karur Vysya Bank	12.61	8.71	
Kotak Mah. Bank	13.23	13.91	
Lakshmi Vilas Bank	14.39	12.06	
Oriental Bank	0	-23.21	
Punjab & Sind Bank	3.89	-14.82	
Punjab National Bank	3.6	-17.55	
South India Bank	9.44	14.90	
State Bank of India	6.97	2.40	
Syndicate Bank	2.98	-4.59	
UCO Bank	0	-21.70	

Union Bank	2.65	-11.49	
United Bank	3.59	-27.82	
Vijaya Bank	10.67	0.17	
Yes Bank	18.58	15.19	

Table 5.60 shows the forecasted values for ROE for all banks for the financial year ending March 2017. The root mean squared error (RMSE) and the mean absolute error (MAE) confirmed variability in the forecast.

Forecasts showed deviations from actual values mainly due the fact that this study only considered a few selected internal determinants of bank profitability. The study also assumed the dependent and independent variables to linearly vary with each other, which may not necessarily prove true.

Forecasts for ROA were in general more accurate than forecasts for ROE showing lesser deviations from actual values. Forecasts for both ROA and ROE were more accurate for profitable banks when compared to their loss making counterparts. This is probably due to the fact that loss making banks had rapidly declining asset quality which proved to be the most influential determinant of both ROA and ROE.

CHAPTER 6

FINDINGS AND CONCLUSION

CHAPTER VI

FINDINGS AND CONCLUSION

6.1 Summary

This research study attempted to examine the profitability of listed commercial banks in India. The study looked at the impact of some key determinants on profitability of listed public and private sector banks in India over a 10 year period. 24 listed public sector banks and 16 listed private sector banks were considered for the study that covered the period from the financial year ending March 2006 to the financial year ending March 2015.

Bank profitability was measured by the return on assets (ROA) and the return on equity (ROE). The determinants of profitability studied were measures of size, asset quality, capital adequacy, income, productivity and lending. Scatter plots, correlation and regression analysis were used to analyze the impact of these determinants on bank profitability. Multivariate models developed were used to generate forecasts for the years ending March 2016 and March 2017. The key findings are as follows:

6.2 Findings

The findings observed are organized into different sub sections. The first sub section compares the profitability of public and private sector banks. The second sub section discusses the impact of asset quality on bank profitability. The third sub section looks at the effect of capital adequacy on the profitability of banks. The next sub section describes at the impact of bank size on profitability. The fifth sub section looks at the impact of productivity on bank profitability. The next sub section looks at the effect of income generation on the profitability of banks. The seventh sub section looks at the impact of lending activity on bank profitability and the last sub section discusses forecasting bank profitability from the key determinants studied.

6.2.1 Comparison of the Profitability of Public and Private Sector banks

Private sector banks were significantly more profitable on the basis of the return on assets than their public sector peers, largely because private sector banks have improved and maintained their asset quality over time when compared to their public counterparts.

Public sector banks were more profitable on the basis of the return on equity than public sector banks. This is because private sector banks regularly access the capital market through equity issuances and consequently face dilution of their equity base while public sector banks are largely dependent on the government for cash infusions.

6.2.2 Impact of Asset Quality on Bank Profitability

Private sector banks had significantly better asset quality than their public sector counterparts. This is mainly because private sector banks have largely avoided lending to problem segments in the economy and have streamlined their asset quality. Asset quality proved to be the most influential determinant of bank profitability. A measure of asset quality percentage Net NPA, negatively impacted profitability as measured by the return on assets and return on equity. Zarrouk et al., (2016) similarly found that asset quality was a key determinant of profitability of a sample of 51 Islamic banks in the Middle East and North Africa (MENA) region.

6.2.3 Impact of Capital Adequacy on Bank Profitability

Private sector banks were significantly more capitalized than their public sector counterparts chiefly because private sector banks have improved their asset quality over time and accessed the capital market more frequently than public sector banks. Capital adequacy positively impacted bank profitability as measured by both the return on assets and the return on equity. While examining a sample of Indonesian banks from 1990-2005, Sufian & Habibullah, (2010) also found that highly capitalized banks were more profitable.

6.2.4 Impact of Bank Size on Bank Profitability

Private sector banks were significantly larger than public sector banks when compared on the basis of stock market capitalization. Hence private sector banks have created much more shareholder value over time when compared to public sector banks. Bank size significantly positively impacted profitability as measured by the return on assets but did not impact profitability as measured by the return on equity. Dietrich and Wanzenried, (2011) similarly observed a positive impact of stock market capitalization on bank profitability when studying 453 banks in Switzerland from 1999 to 2008.

6.2.5 Impact of Productivity on Bank Profitability

Public sector banks were significantly more productive than private sector banks. Productivity negatively impacted profitability as measured by the return on assets and return on equity. A very high productivity of the work force may result in aggressive lending and ultimately lower asset quality which in turn could result in lower return on assets and return on equity. This has been the case for public sector banks in India which have had a higher productivity than their private counterparts.

6.2.6 Impact of Income Generation on Bank Profitability

Private sector banks demonstrated better interest income generation capabilities when compared to public sector banks. This is because private sector banks have optimized their lending while improving and maintaining their asset quality when compared to their public sector peers. Interest income measures impacted bank profitability as measured by the return on assets positively but did not impact profitability as measured by the return on equity. Interest income is the major source of income for most banks. Ganesan, (2001) also found this to be true for a large sample of public sector banks in India studied over a 4 year period.

Private sector banks also demonstrated better noninterest income generation capabilities than public sector banks. This is because private sector banks have diversified their income sources without compromising their asset quality when compared to public sector banks. Noninterest income to average working funds positively impacted bank profitability as measured by both the return on assets and the return on equity positively. Sufian, (2009) similarly observed that Malaysian banks that obtained a greater proportion of their income from noninterest sources were much more profitable.

6.2.7 Impact of Lending Activity on Bank Profitability

While there were no differences in the levels of lending of private and public sector banks, lending measures negatively impacted bank profitability as measured by the return on assets but positively impacted bank profitability as measured by the return on equity. Dhanabhakyam and Kavitha, (2012) similarly found that the credit deposit ratio was an important determinant of bank profitability for a sample of public sector banks, studied in the period between 2001 and 2010.

6.2.8 Forecasting

Forecasts for ROA were in general more accurate than forecasts for ROE showing lesser deviations from actual values. Forecasts for both ROA and ROE were more accurate for profitable banks when compared to their loss making counterparts. This is probably due to the fact that loss making banks had rapidly declining asset quality which proved to be the most influential determinant of both ROA and ROE. Forecasts showed deviations from actual values mainly due the fact that this study only considered a few selected internal determinants of bank profitability. The study also assumed the dependent and independent variables to linearly vary with each other, which may not necessarily prove true, thereby impacting forecast accuracy.

6.3 Implications of the Study

The following are the implications of the study for several key stake holders of banks such as bank managers, investors and the RBI:

6.3.1 Implications for Bankers

- Bank managers can focus on asset quality and control non-performing assets to maximize ROA and ROE
- Bank managers can also ensure their banks are well capitalized and maximize their capital adequacy levels ahead of industry norms to increase their ROA.
- Bank managers could focus on diversifying their income streams with noninterest income sources such as fee based incomes to generate higher ROA's.
- Bank managers could also optimize their lending activity as a function of their deposit base to generate higher ROE's.

6.3.2 Implications for Investors

- To identify banks that are highly profitable investors can focus on banks with very high asset quality.
- Investors can also focus on banks with a diversified income base consisting of interest and noninterest income sources such as fee based income.
- Investors can also identify banks that are well capitalized that have capital adequacy levels well in excess of industry norms.

6.3.3 Implications for Regulators

- The RBI can continue to tighten asset quality norms to help banks identify problem assets well in advance.
- The RBI can require banks to have a robust loan recovery process for identified problem loans, to enable banks to maintain and improve their profitability.

- With the implementation of Basel III norms, the RBI can ensure that banks are well capitalized and have capital adequacy levels in excess of Basel III requirements.

6.4 Scope for Future Research

More exhaustive work can be undertaken by including the impact of additional determinants of bank profitability. The impact of additional measures of capital adequacy, asset quality, managerial efficiency, earnings quality, liquidity, concentration, macroeconomic variables and qualitative measures such as customer tastes and preferences, may be considered on bank profitability measures to make forecasting models more robust. Additionally nonlinear relationships between measures of profitability and key determinants can be incorporated in forecasting models to further improve forecasting efficiency

6.5 Conclusion

This study focused on the impact of some key internal determinants of profitability on the profitability of listed commercial banks in India. The measures of profitability used in the study were the return on assets (ROA) and the return on equity (ROE). The internal determinants selected were bank size as measured by market capitalization, a lending measure namely the deposit to credit ratio, income measures covering interest income to average working funds and noninterest income to average working funds, a key productivity measure in business per employee, a measure of capital adequacy which is the capital adequacy ratio and a measure of asset quality as determined by the percentage Net NPA.

Measures of size, asset quality, capital adequacy, income and lending proved to be influential determinants of profitability as measured by the return on assets and return on equity. Productivity measures had a negative impact on both ROA and ROE. Useful models have been developed to help forecast profitability as measured by the return on assets and return on equity from key determinants.

Thus bank managers must focus on asset quality, improve their capital adequacy and diversify their revenue streams to improve profitability. Investors can focus on these parameters to identify highly profitable banks. The RBI can monitor these parameters as they seek to help banks overcome the ever present challenges of asset quality and capital adequacy in today's ever changing banking landscape.

Bibliography

Journal Articles

1) Ali, M. B., & Chowdhury, T. A. (2010). Effect of Dividend on Stock Price in Emerging Stock Market: A Study on the Listed Private Commercial Banks in DSE. International Journal of Economics and Finance, 2(4), 52–64.
2) Ayadi, N., & Boujelbene, Y. (2012). The Determinants of the Profitability of the Tunisian Deposit Banks. IBIMA Business Review Journal, 2012, 1–21.
3) Beccalli, E., Casu, B., & Girardone, C. (2006). Efficiency and Stock Performance in European Banking. Journal of Business Finance & Accounting, 33(1-2), 245–262.
4) Bodla, B., & Verma, R. (2006). Determinants of Profitability of Banks in India: A Multivariate Analysis. Journal of Services Research, 6(2). 75-89.
5) Chirwa, E. W. (2003). Determinants of commercial banks' profitability in Malawi: a cointegration approach. Applied Financial Economics, 13(8), 565–571.
6) Chronopoulos, D. K., Liu, H., McMillan, F. J., & Wilson, J. O. S. (2013). The dynamics of US bank profitability. The European Journal of Finance, 21(5), 426-443.
7) Chu, S. F., & Lim, G. H. (1998). Share performance and profit efficiency of banks in an oligopolistic market: evidence from Singapore. Journal of Multinational Financial Management.8, 155–168.
8) Dhanabhakyam, M., & Kavitha, M. (2012). Financial performance of selected public sector banks in india. International Journal of Multidisciplinary Research, 2(1), 225-269.
9) Dietrich, A., & Wanzenried, G. (2011). Determinants of bank profitability before and during the crisis: Evidence from Switzerland. Journal of International Financial Markets, Institutions and Money, 21(3), 307–327.

10) Ganesan, P. (2001). Determinants of profits and profitability of public sector banks in India: a profit function approach. Journal of Financial Management and Analysis.14:27-37.
11) Garza-Garcia, J. G. (2012). Does market power influence bank profits in Mexico? A study on market power and efficiency. Applied Financial Economics, 22(1), 21–32.
12) Ghauri, S. M. K. (2014). Determinants of changes in share prices in banking sector of Pakistan. Journal of Economic and Administrative Sciences, 30(2), 121–130.
13) Growe, G., DeBruine, M., Lee, J. and Tudón Maldonado, J. (2014). The Profitability and Performance Measurement of U.S. Regional Banks Using the Predictive Focus of the "Fundamental Analysis Research". Advances in Management Accounting, pp.189-237.
14) Goddard, J., Molyneux, P., & Wilson, J. (2004). Dynamics of growth and profitability in banking. Journal of Money, Credit and Banking, 36(6), 1069–1090.
15) Holden, K., & El-Bannany, M. (2004). Investment in information technology systems and other determinants of bank profitability in the UK. Applied Financial Economics, 14(5), 361–365.
16) Liu, H., & Wilson, J. O. S. (2010). The profitability of banks in Japan. Applied Financial Economics, 20(24), 1851–1866.
17) Masood, O., & Ashraf, M. (2012). Bank-specific and macroeconomic profitability determinants of Islamic banks: The case of different countries. Qualitative Research in Financial Markets, 4(2/3), 255–268.
18) Menaje, P. M. (2012). Impact of Selected Financial Variables on Share Price of Publicly Listed Firms in the Philippines. American International Journal of Contemporary Research, 2(9), 98–104.
19) Miller, S. M., & Noulas, A. G. (1997). Portfolio mix and large-bank profitability in the USA. Applied Economics, 29(4), 505–512.

20) Molyneux, P., & Forbes, W. (1995). Market structure and performance in European banking. Applied Economics, 27(2), 155–159.
21) Molyneux, P., & Thornton, J. (1992). Determinants of European bank profitability: A note. Journal of Banking and Finance, 16(6), 1173–1178.
22) Naceur, S. B., & Goaied, M. (2001). The determinants of the Tunisian deposit banks' performance. Applied Financial Economics, 11(3), 317–319.
23) Seetharaman, A., & Raj, J. R. (2011). An Empirical Study on the Impact of Earnings per Share on Stock Prices of a Listed Bank in Malaysia. The International Journal of Applied Economics and Finance, 5(2), 114–126.
24) Sensarma, R., & Jayadev, M. (2009). Are bank stocks sensitive to risk management? The Journal of Risk Finance, 10(1), 7–22.
25) Singh, P. (2006). A Study on Banks Performance in India: Fundamentals versus Stock Market. Asia-Pacific Journal of Management Research and Innovation, 2(1), 55–64.
26) Smirlock, M., & Brown, D. (1986). Collusion, Efficiency and Pricing Behavior: Evidence from the Banking Industry. Economic Inquiry, 24(1), 85–96.
27) Sufian, F. (2009). Factors Influencing Bank Profitability in a Developing Economy: Empirical Evidence from Malaysia. Global Business Review, 10(2), 225–241.
28) Sufian, F., & Habibullah, M. S. (2010). Assessing the Impact of Financial Crisis on Bank Performance: Empirical Evidence from Indonesia. ASEAN Economic Bulletin, 27, 245-262.
29) Sufian, F., & Habibullah, M. S. (2009). Bank specific and macroeconomic determinants of bank profitability: Empirical evidence from the China banking sector. Frontiers of Economics in China, 4(2), 274–291.
30) Tan, Y., & Floros, C. (2012). Bank Profitability and Inflation: The Case of China. Journal of Economic Studies, 39(6), 675–696.
31) Thiagarajan, S., Ayyapan, S., & Ramachandran, A. (2011). An Analysis of Determinants of Profitability in Public and Private Sector Banks in India. Resarch Journal of Social Science & Management, 1(06), 140–152.

32) Uddin, M. B. (2009). Determinants of market price of stock: A study on bank leasing and insurance companies of Bangladesh. Journal of Modern Accounting and Auditing, 5(7), 1–7.
33) Vyas, R. K., Singh, M., & Yadav, R. (2008). The Impact of Capital Adequacy Requirements on Performance of Scheduled Commercial Banks. Asia-Pacific Journal of Management Research and Innovation, 4(2), 74–81.
34) Zarrouk, H., Jedidia, K. Ben, & Moualhi, M. (2016). Is Islamic bank profitability driven by same forces as conventional banks? International Journal of Islamic and Middle Eastern Finance and Management, 9(1), 46–66.

Books

1) Hoggson, N. F. (1926) Banking Through the Ages, New York, Dodd, Mead & Company.
2) Kothari, C. and Garg, G. (2014). Research methodology Methods and Techniques. 3rd ed. New Delhi: New Age International (P) Ltd.
3) Suresh, P., & Paul, J. (2014). Management of Banking and Financial Services. 3rd ed. Pearson India.

Web Sites

1) 15 Types of Regression you should know. Retrieved from https://www.r-bloggers.com/15-types-of-regression-you-should-know, Accessed, 06 May. 2018
2) Banking Structure in India – IMS. Retrieved from http://myimsv2.imsindia.com/2016/05/28/banking-structure-in-india, Accessed, 06 May. 2018
3) Correlation Coefficient: Simple Definition, Formula, Easy Steps. Retrieved from http://www.statisticshowto.com/probability-and-statistics/correlation-coefficient-formula, Accessed, 06 May. 2018
4) Damodaran, A. (2018). Statistical Distributions. Retrieved from http://people.stern.nyu.edu/adamodar/New_Home_Page/StatFile/statdistns.html, Accessed, 24 May. 2018.

5) In charts: How bad really is India's bad loans problem? Retrieved from https://www.vccircle.com/in-charts-how-bad-really-is-indias-bad-loans-problem, Accessed, 24 May. 2018
6) Private Sector Banks. Retrieved from https://www.moneycontrol.com/competition/icicibank/comparison/ICI02#ICI02, Accessed, 21 May. 2018
7) Public Sector Banks. Retrieved from https://www.moneycontrol.com/competition/statebankindia/comparison/SBI#SBI, Accessed, 21 May. 2018
8) Reserve Bank of India - Chronology of Events. Retrieved from https://www.rbi.org.in/scripts/chro_1968.aspx, Accessed, 14 Feb. 2018.
9) Singh, H. Structure of Banking Sector in India. Retrieved from https://www.jagranjosh.com/general-knowledge/structure-of-banking-sector-in-india-1448530019-1, Accessed, 06 May. 2018
10) T Test (Student's T-Test): Definition and Examples. Retrieved from http://www.statisticshowto.com/probability-and-statistics/t-test, Accessed, 06 May. 2018
11) The Advent of Modern Banking in India. Retrieved from https://rbi.org.in/Scripts/ms_banks.aspx, Accessed, 14 Feb. 2018.
12) Trend and Progress of Banking in India. (2017). Retrieved from https://www.rbi.org.in/scripts/AnnualPublications.aspx?head=Trend%20and%20Progress%20of%20Banking%20in%20India, Accessed, 14 Feb. 2018.
13) What is Basel III? - Quora. Retrieved from https://www.quora.com/What-is-Basel-III, Accessed, 06 May. 2018
14) http://www.zeebiz.com
15) https://cmie.com

Annexures

Annexure 1

Descriptive Statistics

Summary Statistics, using the observations 1 - 387
for the variable ROA (387 valid observations)

Mean	Median	Minimum	Maximum
0.93295	0.92000	-2.0100	2.5000
Std. Dev.	C.V.	Skewness	Ex. kurtosis
0.54721	0.58654	-1.2528	5.3376
5% Perc.	95% Perc.	IQ range	Missing obs.
0.23000	1.7320	0.65000	0

Summary Statistics, using the observations 1 - 387
for the variable ROE (387 valid observations)

Mean	Median	Minimum	Maximum
15.184	16.040	-51.880	31.600
Std. Dev.	C.V.	Skewness	Ex. kurtosis
7.7130	0.50796	-2.2355	16.040
5% Perc.	95% Perc.	IQ range	Missing obs.
4.0680	25.912	9.0600	0

Summary Statistics, using the observations 1 - 387
for the variable S (387 valid observations)

Mean	Median	Minimum	Maximum
16132.	4622.4	99.710	2.5638e+005
Std. Dev.	C.V.	Skewness	Ex. kurtosis
33710.	2.0896	3.7233	15.293
5% Perc.	95% Perc.	IQ range	Missing obs.

| 664.02 | 1.0124e+005 | 9118.9 | 0 |

Summary Statistics, using the observations 1 - 387
for the variable CAR (387 valid observations)

Mean	Median	Minimum	Maximum
13.227	12.890	9.2100	24.110
Std. Dev.	C.V.	Skewness	Ex. kurtosis
2.1397	0.16176	1.6220	4.0266
5% Perc.	95% Perc.	IQ range	Missing obs.
10.698	17.628	2.0800	0

Summary Statistics, using the observations 1 - 387
for the variable BPE (387 valid observations)

Mean	Median	Minimum	Maximum
9.1773	8.3700	2.7700	26.210
Std. Dev.	C.V.	Skewness	Ex. kurtosis
4.3762	0.47685	1.0645	1.3474
5% Perc.	95% Perc.	IQ range	Missing obs.
3.6780	17.330	5.7900	0

Summary Statistics, using the observations 1 - 387
for the variable DCR (387 valid observations)

Mean	Median	Minimum	Maximum
138.16	138.64	41.878	189.43
Std. Dev.	C.V.	Skewness	Ex. kurtosis
16.418	0.11883	-0.85189	4.4208
5% Perc.	95% Perc.	IQ range	Missing obs.
107.93	165.23	16.770	0

Summary Statistics, using the observations 1 - 387

for the variable NNPA (387 valid observations)

Mean	Median	Minimum	Maximum
1.3234	1.0100	0.010000	7.1800
Std. Dev.	C.V.	Skewness	Ex. kurtosis
1.0515	0.79452	1.5967	3.8457
5% Perc.	95% Perc.	IQ range	Missing obs.
0.18000	3.3600	1.3100	0

Summary Statistics, using the observations 1 - 387
for the variable IIAWF (387 valid observations)

Mean	Median	Minimum	Maximum
8.6009	8.5200	6.5100	11.440
Std. Dev.	C.V.	Skewness	Ex. kurtosis
0.94778	0.11020	0.12909	-0.60608
5% Perc.	95% Perc.	IQ range	Missing obs.
7.1180	10.206	1.3900	0

Summary Statistics, using the observations 1 - 387
for the variable NIIAWF (387 valid observations)

Mean	Median	Minimum	Maximum
1.1811	1.0800	0.46000	2.8500
Std. Dev.	C.V.	Skewness	Ex. kurtosis
0.44982	0.38084	1.0476	0.79699
5% Perc.	95% Perc.	IQ range	Missing obs.
0.62000	2.0900	0.52000	0

Annexure 2

Correlation Matrix

Correlation coefficients, using the observations 1 - 387
5% critical value (two-tailed) = 0.0997 for n = 387

ROA	ROE	S	CAR	BPE	
1.0000	0.6954	0.3001	0.4992	-0.1102	ROA
	1.0000	0.0376	0.1996	-0.1404	ROE
		1.0000	0.3389	0.0196	S
			1.0000	-0.0206	CAR
				1.0000	BPE

DCR	NNPA	IIAWF	NIIAWF	
-0.1956	-0.6830	0.1786	0.4124	ROA
0.0364	-0.6772	-0.0046	0.0739	ROE
-0.3739	-0.0821	-0.1040	0.3675	S
-0.3316	-0.3517	0.2153	0.3750	CAR
-0.3375	0.2537	0.2185	-0.2322	BPE
1.0000	0.0123	-0.2444	-0.2469	DCR
	1.0000	0.0422	-0.3356	NNPA
		1.0000	-0.0009	IIAWF
			1.0000	NIIAWF

Annexure 3

Ordinary Least Squares ROA as a Function of All Variables

Model 1: OLS, using observations 1-387

Dependent variable: ROA

Heteroskedasticity-robust standard errors, variant HC1

	Coefficient	Std. Error	t-ratio	p-value	
Const	0.541807	0.383495	1.413	0.1585	
NNPA	−0.302074	0.0391252	−7.721	<0.0001	***
CAR	0.0522953	0.0129980	4.023	<0.0001	***
NIIAWF	0.116413	0.0643848	1.808	0.0714	*
S	2.21021e-06	5.30391e-07	4.167	<0.0001	***
DCR	−0.000960223	0.00163101	−0.5887	0.5564	
BPE	0.00639619	0.00408373	1.566	0.1181	

Mean dependent var	0.932946	S.D. dependent var	0.547214
Sum squared resid	48.67799	S.E. of regression	0.357911
R-squared	0.578856	Adjusted R-squared	0.572207
F(6, 380)	58.86511	P-value(F)	2.52e-51
Log-likelihood	−147.9654	Akaike criterion	309.9309
Schwarz criterion	337.6398	Hannan-Quinn	320.9182

Annexure 4

Ordinary Least Squares ROA as a Function of Significant Variables

Model 2: OLS, using observations 1-387

Dependent variable: ROA

	Coefficient	Std. Error	t-ratio	p-value	
Const	0.498499	0.137533	3.625	0.0003	***
NNPA	−0.305176	0.0186588	−16.36	<0.0001	***
CAR	0.0599649	0.00971355	6.173	<0.0001	***
S	2.79925e-06	5.79115e-07	4.834	<0.0001	***

Mean dependent var	0.932946	S.D. dependent var	0.547214
Sum squared resid	49.78017	S.E. of regression	0.360520
R-squared	0.569321	Adjusted R-squared	0.565947
$F(3, 383)$	168.7643	P-value(F)	1.03e-69
Log-likelihood	−152.2979	Akaike criterion	312.5957
Schwarz criterion	328.4294	Hannan-Quinn	318.8742

Annexure 5

Tests for Heteroskedasticity and Normality of Residuals

Breusch-Pagan test for heteroskedasticity -

Null hypothesis: heteroskedasticity not present

Test statistic: LM = 156.293

with p-value = P(Chi-square(3) > 156.293) = 1.15631e-033

Test for normality of residual -

Null hypothesis: error is normally distributed

Test statistic: Chi-square (2) = 208.625

with p-value = 4.98606e-046

Annexure 6

Univariate Quantile Regression Analysis ROA as a Function of Independent Variables

Model 1: LAD, using observations 1-387
Dependent variable: ROA

	Coefficient	Std. Error	t-ratio	p-value	
Const	0.862847	0.0287243	30.04	<0.0001	***
S	6.22986e-06	9.76896e-07	6.377	<0.0001	***

Median depend. Var	0.920000	S.D. dependent var	0.547214
Sum absolute resid	148.8536	Sum squared resid	106.3466
Log-likelihood	−285.4844	Akaike criterion	574.9687

Schwarz criterion	582.8856	Hannan-Quinn	578.1079	

Model 2: Quantile estimates, using observations 1-387

Dependent variable: ROA

tau = 0.5

Asymptotic standard errors assuming IID errors

	Coefficient	Std. Error	t-ratio	p-value	
Const	−0.885676	0.111666	−7.931	<0.0001	***
CAR	0.138514	0.00833410	16.62	<0.0001	***

Median depend. Var	0.920000	S.D. dependent var	0.547214
Sum absolute resid	126.6367	Sum squared resid	87.06442
Log-likelihood	−222.9293	Akaike criterion	449.8586
Schwarz criterion	457.7755	Hannan-Quinn	452.9979

Model 3: Quantile estimates, using observations 1-387

Dependent variable: ROA

tau = 0.5

Asymptotic standard errors assuming IID errors

	Coefficient	Std. Error	t-ratio	p-value	
const	1.21324	0.0794147	15.28	<0.0001	***
BPE	−0.0294906	0.00781264	−3.775	0.0002	***

Median depend. Var	0.920000	S.D. dependent var	0.547214
Sum absolute resid	151.8242	Sum squared resid	116.0446
Log-likelihood	−293.1316	Akaike criterion	590.2632
Schwarz criterion	598.1801	Hannan-Quinn	593.4024

Model 4: Quantile estimates, using observations 1-387
Dependent variable: ROA
tau = 0.5
Asymptotic standard errors assuming IID errors

	Coefficient	Std. Error	t-ratio	p-value	
const	1.58472	0.281191	5.636	<0.0001	***
DCR	−0.00469204	0.00202115	−2.321	0.0208	**

Median depend. Var	0.920000	S.D. dependent var	0.547214
Sum absolute resid	155.5710	Sum squared resid	111.5164
Log-likelihood	−302.5662	Akaike criterion	609.1323
Schwarz criterion	617.0492	Hannan-Quinn	612.2715

Model 5: Quantile estimates, using observations 1-387
Dependent variable: ROA
tau = 0.5
Asymptotic standard errors assuming IID errors

	Coefficient	Std. Error	t-ratio	p-value	
const	1.38743	0.0283931	48.86	<0.0001	***
NNPA	−0.346535	0.0168060	−20.62	<0.0001	***

Median depend. var	0.920000	S.D. dependent var	0.547214
Sum absolute resid	106.8490	Sum squared resid	61.70124
Log-likelihood	−157.1759	Akaike criterion	318.3517
Schwarz criterion	326.2686	Hannan-Quinn	321.4910

Model 6: Quantile estimates, using observations 1-387
Dependent variable: ROA
tau = 0.5
Asymptotic standard errors assuming IID errors

	Coefficient	Std. Error	t-ratio	p-value	
const	0.0379470	0.253591	0.1496	0.8811	
IIAWF	0.109272	0.0293073	3.728	0.0002	***

Median depend. var	0.920000	S.D. dependent var	0.547214
Sum absolute resid	153.7929	Sum squared resid	112.6876
Log-likelihood	−298.1176	Akaike criterion	600.2352
Schwarz criterion	608.1520	Hannan-Quinn	603.3744

Model 7: Quantile estimates, using observations 1-387
Dependent variable: ROA
tau = 0.5
Asymptotic standard errors assuming IID errors

	Coefficient	Std. Error	t-ratio	p-value	
const	0.259677	0.0653471	3.974	<0.0001	***
NIIAWF	0.607527	0.0517126	11.75	<0.0001	***

Median depend. var	0.920000	S.D. dependent var	0.547214
Sum absolute resid	132.1801	Sum squared resid	97.55958
Log-likelihood	−239.5095	Akaike criterion	483.0189
Schwarz criterion	490.9358	Hannan-Quinn	486.1582

Annexure 7

Multi-variate Quantile Regression Analysis ROA as a Function of Independent Variables

Model 4: Quantile estimates, using observations 1-387

Dependent variable: ROA

tau = 0.5

Asymptotic standard errors assuming IID errors

	Coefficient	Std. Error	t-ratio	p-value	
Const	−0.321749	0.257278	−1.251	0.2119	
NNPA	−0.286551	0.0150410	−19.05	<0.0001	***
CAR	0.0383612	0.00796225	4.818	<0.0001	***
S	2.64685e-06	4.91075e-07	5.390	<0.0001	***
BPE	−0.00218546	0.00369056	−0.5922	0.5541	
DCR	0.00129428	0.00104994	1.233	0.2184	
IIAWF	0.0872498	0.0161239	5.411	<0.0001	***
NIIAWF	0.170657	0.0373657	4.567	<0.0001	***

Median depend. var	0.920000	S.D. dependent var	0.547214
Sum absolute resid	84.28382	Sum squared resid	46.57393
Log-likelihood	−65.36910	Akaike criterion	146.7382

Schwarz criterion   178.4056   Hannan-Quinn   159.2951

Test for normality of residual -

Null hypothesis: error is normally distributed

Test statistic: Chi-square (2) = 170.725

with p-value = 8.46461e-038

Variance Inflation Factors

Minimum possible value = 1.0

Values > 10.0 may indicate a collinearity problem

Model 6: Quantile estimates, using observations 1-387

Dependent variable: ROA

tau = 0.25

Asymptotic standard errors assuming IID errors

	Coefficient	Std. Error	t-ratio	p-value	
const	−0.315572	0.181620	−1.738	0.0831	*
NNPA	−0.272155	0.0181464	−15.00	<0.0001	***
CAR	0.0426025	0.00964918	4.415	<0.0001	***
S	2.62835e-06	5.74899e-07	4.572	<0.0001	***
IIAWF	0.0810894	0.0190074	4.266	<0.0001	***

NIIAWF	0.141922	0.0441179	3.217	0.0014	***

Median depend. var	0.920000	S.D. dependent var	0.547214
Sum absolute resid	101.1197	Sum squared resid	53.39977
Log-likelihood	−128.8041	Akaike criterion	269.6082
Schwarz criterion	293.3587	Hannan-Quinn	279.0259

Model 5: Quantile estimates, using observations 1-387

Dependent variable: ROA

tau = 0.5

Robust (sandwich) standard errors

	Coefficient	Std. Error	t-ratio	p-value	
const	−0.0484360	0.144445	−0.3353	0.7376	
NNPA	−0.293475	0.0156933	−18.70	<0.0001	***
CAR	0.0382100	0.00684636	5.581	<0.0001	***
S	2.59219e-06	4.18801e-07	6.190	<0.0001	***
IIAWF	0.0762347	0.0151494	5.032	<0.0001	***
NIIAWF	0.163528	0.0383988	4.259	<0.0001	***

Median depend. var	0.920000	S.D. dependent var	0.547214

Sum absolute resid	84.51242	Sum squared resid	46.23180
Log-likelihood	−66.41731	Akaike criterion	144.8346
Schwarz criterion	168.5852	Hannan-Quinn	154.2523

Model 7: Quantile estimates, using observations 1-387

Dependent variable: ROA

tau = 0.75

Robust (sandwich) standard errors

	Coefficient	Std. Error	t-ratio	p-value	
const	−0.328294	0.157663	−2.082	0.0380	**
NNPA	−0.248604	0.0182173	−13.65	<0.0001	***
CAR	0.0409535	0.00339790	12.05	<0.0001	***
S	1.61483e-06	4.44155e-07	3.636	0.0003	***
IIAWF	0.106343	0.0168314	6.318	<0.0001	***
NIIAWF	0.238014	0.0411564	5.783	<0.0001	***

Median depend. var	0.920000	S.D. dependent var	0.547214
Sum absolute resid	99.46329	Sum squared resid	59.11854
Log-likelihood	−81.68919	Akaike criterion	175.3784
Schwarz criterion	199.1289	Hannan-Quinn	184.7960

Annexure 8

Multi-variate Quantile Regression Analysis ROA as a Function of Significant Independent Variables

Model 1: Quantile estimates, using observations 1-387
Dependent variable: ROA
tau = 0.5
Robust (sandwich) standard errors

	Coefficient	Std. Error	t-ratio	p-value	
Const	−0.130459	0.163308	−0.7988	0.4249	
CAR	0.0553797	0.00859721	6.442	<0.0001	***
NNPA	−0.278430	0.0163911	−16.99	<0.0001	***
IIAWF	0.0582868	0.0166763	3.495	0.0005	***
NIIAWF	0.183913	0.0386372	4.760	<0.0001	***

Median depend. var	0.920000	S.D. dependent var	0.547214
Sum absolute resid	88.31662	Sum squared resid	49.09474
Log-likelihood	−83.45686	Akaike criterion	176.9137
Schwarz criterion	196.7058	Hannan-Quinn	184.7618

Annexure 9

Ordinary Least Squares ROE as a Function of All Variables

Model 10: OLS, using observations 1-387

Dependent variable: ROE

	Coefficient	Std. Error	t-ratio	p-value	
Const	21.3154	5.23684	4.070	<0.0001	***
NNPA	−5.44126	0.306158	−17.77	<0.0001	***
CAR	−0.0448588	0.162070	−0.2768	0.7821	
S	1.49847e-05	9.99576e-06	1.499	0.1347	
IIAWF	0.348943	0.328199	1.063	0.2884	
NIIAWF	−3.17665	0.760572	−4.177	<0.0001	***
BPE	0.00834873	0.0751207	0.1111	0.9116	
DCR	0.0151697	0.0213714	0.7098	0.4783	

Mean dependent var	15.18429	S.D. dependent var	7.712964
Sum squared resid	11734.92	S.E. of regression	5.564427
R-squared	0.488966	Adjusted R-squared	0.479527
$F(7, 379)$	51.80472	P-value(F)	1.46e-51

Log-likelihood −1209.332	Akaike criterion	2434.664
Schwarz criterion 2466.331	Hannan-Quinn	2447.220

Annexure 10

Ordinary Least Squares ROE as a Function of Significant Variables

Model 11: OLS, using observations 1-387

Dependent variable: ROE

	Coefficient	Std. Error	t-ratio	p-value	
const	25.8200	1.02031	25.31	<0.0001	***
NNPA	−5.39279	0.285126	−18.91	<0.0001	***
NIIAWF	−2.96219	0.666517	−4.444	<0.0001	***

Mean dependent var	15.18429	S.D. dependent var	7.712964
Sum squared resid	11823.21	S.E. of regression	5.548838
R-squared	0.485121	Adjusted R-squared	0.482439
$F_{(2, 384)}$	180.9029	P-value(F)	4.44e-56
Log-likelihood	−1210.782	Akaike criterion	2427.564
Schwarz criterion	2439.440	Hannan-Quinn	2432.273

Annexure 11

Tests for Heteroskedasticity and Normality of Residuals

Breusch-Pagan test for heteroskedasticity -

Null hypothesis: heteroskedasticity not present

Test statistic: LM = 148.34

with p-value = P(Chi-square(2) > 148.34) = 6.14212e-033

Test for normality of residual -

Null hypothesis: error is normally distributed

Test statistic: Chi-square (2) = 188.906

with p-value = 9.5417e-042

Annexure 12

Univariate Quantile Regression Analysis ROA as a Function of Independent Variables

Model 8: Quantile estimates, using observations 1-387
Dependent variable: ROE
tau = 0.5
Asymptotic standard errors assuming IID errors

	Coefficient	Std. Error	t-ratio	p-value	
const	16.1081	0.578500	27.84	<0.0001	***
S	−4.78264e−06	1.54962e−05	−0.3086	0.7578	

Median depend. var	16.04000	S.D. dependent var	7.712964
Sum absolute resid	2162.017	Sum squared resid	23286.65
Log-likelihood	−1321.032	Akaike criterion	2646.064
Schwarz criterion	2653.981	Hannan-Quinn	2649.203

Model 1: Quantile estimates, using observations 1-387
Dependent variable: ROE
tau = 0.5
Asymptotic standard errors assuming IID errors

	Coefficient	Std. Error	t-ratio	p-value	
const	18.9114	0.929614	20.34	<0.0001	***
BPE	−0.375683	0.0914533	−4.108	<0.0001	***

Median depend. var	16.04000	S.D. dependent var	7.712964
Sum absolute resid	2094.564	Sum squared resid	22661.80
Log-likelihood	−1308.766	Akaike criterion	2621.531
Schwarz criterion	2629.448	Hannan-Quinn	2624.671

Model 9: Quantile estimates, using observations 1-387
Dependent variable: ROE
tau = 0.5
Asymptotic standard errors assuming IID errors

	Coefficient	Std. Error	t-ratio	p-value	
const	9.45112	3.10527	3.044	0.0025	***
CAR	0.470175	0.231759	2.029	0.0432	**

Median depend. var	16.04000	S.D. dependent var	7.712964
Sum absolute resid	2133.138	Sum squared resid	22249.42
Log-likelihood	−1315.828	Akaike criterion	2635.656
Schwarz criterion	2643.572	Hannan-Quinn	2638.795

Model 11: Quantile estimates, using observations 1-387

Dependent variable: ROE

tau = 0.5

Asymptotic standard errors assuming IID errors

	Coefficient	Std. Error	t-ratio	p-value	
const	5.75745	3.10110	1.857	0.0641	*
DCR	0.0743206	0.0222901	3.334	0.0009	***

Median depend. var	16.04000	S.D. dependent var	7.712964
Sum absolute resid	2099.567	Sum squared resid	23546.63
Log-likelihood	−1309.689	Akaike criterion	2623.378
Schwarz criterion	2631.294	Hannan-Quinn	2626.517

Model 13: Quantile estimates, using observations 1-387

Dependent variable: ROE

tau = 0.5

Asymptotic standard errors assuming IID errors

	Coefficient	Std. Error	t-ratio	p-value	
const	21.2672	0.461670	46.07	<0.0001	***

NNPA	−4.57402	0.273264	−16.74	<0.0001	***

Median depend. var	16.04000	S.D. dependent var	7.712964
Sum absolute resid	1532.552	Sum squared resid	12497.80
Log-likelihood	−1187.863	Akaike criterion	2379.725
Schwarz criterion	2387.642	Hannan-Quinn	2382.864

Model 14: Quantile estimates, using observations 1-387

Dependent variable: ROE

tau = 0.5

Asymptotic standard errors assuming IID errors

	Coefficient	Std. Error	t-ratio	p-value	
const	22.0802	4.59230	4.808	<0.0001	***
IIAWF	−0.713755	0.530728	−1.345	0.1795	

Median depend. var	16.04000	S.D. dependent var	7.712964
Sum absolute resid	2156.404	Sum squared resid	23342.86
Log-likelihood	−1320.026	Akaike criterion	2644.052
Schwarz criterion	2651.969	Hannan-Quinn	2647.191

Model 15: Quantile estimates, using observations 1-387

Dependent variable: ROE

tau = 0.5

Asymptotic standard errors assuming IID errors

	Coefficient	Std. Error	t-ratio	p-value	
const	13.0560	1.19083	10.96	<0.0001	***
NIIAWF	2.20000	0.942365	2.335	0.0201	**

Median depend. var	16.04000	S.D. dependent var	7.712964
Sum absolute resid	2132.250	Sum squared resid	22990.93
Log-likelihood	−1315.667	Akaike criterion	2635.333
Schwarz criterion	2643.250	Hannan-Quinn	2638.473

Annexure 13

Multi-variate Quantile Regression Analysis ROA as a Function of Independent Variables

Model 12: Quantile estimates, using observations 1-387

Dependent variable: ROE

tau = 0.5

Robust (sandwich) standard errors

	Coefficient	Std. Error	t-ratio	p-value	
Const	17.4781	4.16826	4.193	<0.0001	***
NNPA	−5.11265	0.238597	−21.43	<0.0001	***
NIIAWF	−1.77370	0.620522	−2.858	0.0045	***
S	8.54066e-06	5.69093e-06	1.501	0.1343	
CAR	−0.104107	0.125556	−0.8292	0.4075	
BPE	−0.0140866	0.0449184	−0.3136	0.7540	
DCR	0.0435309	0.0206652	2.106	0.0358	**
IIAWF	0.232107	0.253560	0.9154	0.3606	

Median depend. var	16.04000	S.D. dependent var	7.712964

Sum absolute resid	1482.374	Sum squared resid	11975.85
Log-likelihood	−1174.980	Akaike criterion	2365.959
Schwarz criterion	2397.626	Hannan-Quinn	2378.516

Annexure 14

Multi-variate Quantile Regression Analysis ROA as a Function of Significant Variables

Model 13: Quantile estimates, using observations 1-387

Dependent variable: ROE

tau = 0.5

Asymptotic standard errors assuming IID errors

	Coefficient	Std. Error	t-ratio	p-value	
const	18.8191	2.63314	7.147	<0.0001	***
NNPA	−5.05440	0.260966	−19.37	<0.0001	***
NIIAWF	−1.55803	0.629478	−2.475	0.0138	**
DCR	0.0361263	0.0162481	2.223	0.0268	**

Median depend. var	16.04000	S.D. dependent var	7.712964
Sum absolute resid	1485.642	Sum squared resid	12027.76

Log-likelihood	−1175.832	Akaike criterion	2359.663
Schwarz criterion	2375.497	Hannan-Quinn	2365.942

Model 14: Quantile estimates, using observations 1-387

Dependent variable: ROE

tau = 0.25

Asymptotic standard errors assuming IID errors

	Coefficient	Std. Error	t-ratio	p-value	
const	17.1966	3.59679	4.781	<0.0001	***
NNPA	−4.69299	0.356472	−13.17	<0.0001	***
NIIAWF	−1.09609	0.859849	−1.275	0.2032	
DCR	0.0210726	0.0221944	0.9495	0.3430	

Median depend. var	16.04000	S.D. dependent var	7.712964
Sum absolute resid	1763.289	Sum squared resid	14711.44
Log-likelihood	−1224.543	Akaike criterion	2457.086
Schwarz criterion	2472.920	Hannan-Quinn	2463.364

Model 15: Quantile estimates, using observations 1-387

Dependent variable: ROE

tau = 0.75

Asymptotic standard errors assuming IID errors

	Coefficient	Std. Error	t-ratio	p-value	
const	20.1449	4.58786	4.391	<0.0001	***
NNPA	−4.79255	0.454695	−10.54	<0.0001	***
NIIAWF	−2.46667	1.09677	−2.249	0.0251	**
DCR	0.0571820	0.0283099	2.020	0.0441	**

Median depend. var	16.04000	S.D. dependent var	7.712964
Sum absolute resid	1890.325	Sum squared resid	17277.93
Log-likelihood	−1202.215	Akaike criterion	2412.430
Schwarz criterion	2428.263	Hannan-Quinn	2418.708

Rajveer Rawlin

Faculty, M.S. Ramaiah Institute of Management
Banking
Stock Markets

GET MY OWN PROFILE

	All	Since 2013
Citations	14	14
h-index	1	1
i10-index	1	1

TITLE	CITED BY	YEAR
Modeling the NPA of a Midsized Indian Nationalized Bank as a Function of Advances R Rawlin, SM Sharan, PB Lakshmipathy European Journal of Business and Management 4 (5), 78-89	11	2012
IMPACT OF KEY INTERNAL DETERMINANTS ON PROFITABILITY AND SHARE PRICE PERFORMANCE OF A LARGE PUBLIC SECTOR BANK IN INDIA R Rawlin, R Shanmugam INTERNATIONAL JOURNAL OF BUSINESS AND ECONOMIC RESEARCH 1 (1), 183-195	1	2013
Do FII Transaction Amounts, F&O Turnover Amounts, & Volatility Influence The Indian Stock Market Index The Nifty? R Rawlin, N Ganesan, Y Priya, S Shekhawat Great Lakes Herald	1	2013
Modeling the NPA of a Large Indian Public Sector Bank as a Function of Total Assets R Rawlin, SM Sharan Dayananda Sagar College of Engineering	1	2011
Comparative Analysis of Top Private Sector Banks in India based on CAMEL Parameters R Rawlin, M Mounika, R Shanmugam		2017
Do Determinants of Bank Profitability Change Over Time? Evidence from India R Rawlin, R Shanmugam		2017
Do Determinants of Bank Stock Price Performance Change Over Time? Evidence from India R Rawlin		2017
Ranking Selected Public Sector Banks in India based on the Camel Rating Methodology R Rawlin, M Singh, R Shanmugam GRIN Verlag		2017
A Comparison of the Effects of Key Determinants on Share Prices of India's Largest Public and Private Sector Banks R Rawlin, R Shanmugam, V Bhat Great Lakes Herald 9 (2), 1-12		2015
A Comparison of Key Determinants on Profitability of India's Largest Public and Private Sector Banks R Rawlin, R Shanmugam, V Bhat		2014

TITLE	CITED BY	YEAR
NON-LINEAR RELATIONSHIPS OF KEY DETERMINANTS IN INFLUENCING THE SHARE PRICE OF INDIA'S LARGEST PUBLIC SECTOR BANK R Rawlin, R Shanmugam International Journal of Economics, Commerce and Management 2 (3)		2014
NON-LINEAR RELATIONSHIPS OF KEY DETERMINANTS IN INFLUENCING THE PROFITABILITY OF A LARGE PUBLIC SECTOR BANK IN INDIA R Rawlin, R Shanmugam Great Lakes Herald 7 (1), 35-40		2013
Modeling the NPA of a Large Public Bank as a Function of Advances R Rawlin, S Sharan The Journal of Contemporary Management Research		2012
Multivariate Analysis to get an Estimate of the Indian Stock Market Nifty Index R Rawlin GRIN Verlag		2011
Do Exotic options offer any specific advantages in Forex trading? R Rawlin University Of Wales Institute, Cardiff		2005

Comparative Analysis of Top Private Sector Banks in India based on CAMEL Parameters

Rajveer S. Rawlin*, Muddam Mounika**, and Ramaswamy Shanmugam***

ABSTRACT

The CAMEL rating is a well-established technique to compare the performance of banks and financial institutions. The Compound Annual Growth Rate (CAGR) is a very useful growth measure. We compare the top five private sector banks in India, ranking them via the CAMEL rating based on the CAGR of CAMEL parameters. Of the banks chosen for the study, IndusInd bank ranked first in capital adequacy, asset quality and earnings quality. HDFC bank ranked first in management efficiency and Axis bank ranked first in liquidity. The bank with the best overall CAMEL rank proved to be IndusInd bank. By providing a basis of comparison for different banks, the CAMEL rating can yield valuable insight to several stake holders of banks such as top management, investors and regulators.

Keywords: *CAMEL rating; Banks; Capital adequacy; Asset quality; Management efficiency; Earnings quality; Liquidity.*

1.0 Introduction

The Indian banking sector has been plagued with the problem of Non-Performing Assets (NPA) for quite some time now. Private banks have seen their stock prices appreciate a lot more than their public counterparts as they have demonstrated much better asset quality in their recent earnings reports. With the recent demonetisation embarked by the government and adoption of international banking norms such as Basel 3 banking margins could come under further pressure.

---

*Corresponding author; Assistant Professor, Ramaiah Institute of Management, Bangalore, Karnataka, India. (Email id: rajveer@msrim.org; samuelrr@yahoo.com)
**Graduate student, Ramaiah Institute of Management, Bangalore, Karnataka, India. (Email id: mounika93m@gmail.com)
*** Visiting Professor, PSG Institute of Management, Coimbatore, Tamil Nadu, India. (Email id: ramshanmugam@yahoo.co.in)

Given the utmost importance of the banking sector to the economy it would prove useful to rate and compare some of India's largest private banks. This study seeks to understand and compare some of India's largest private sector banks via the well-known CAMEL rating system. The CAMEL rating system is an internationally recognized rating system that regulatory authorities use in order to rate and rank financial institutions according to five factors represented by the acronym "CAMEL". These are Capital Adequacy, Asset Quality, Management, Earnings and Liquidity (CAMEL). Each financial institution is assigned a score based on these measures. An overall ranking based on CAMEL parameters is developed. However the CAMEL model when implemented as it is may not provide a true picture of the bank's performance. Hence using performance measures like the Compound Annual Growth Rate (CAGR) in conjunction with the CAMEL rating parameters will yield more representative results. This can help us compare different banks and financial institutions.

Several studies have illustrated the use of the CAMEL rating as a comparison tool. Sangmi and Nazir (2010) used the Camel rating to study the performance of a few banks in India. Misra and Aspal (2013) compared State Bank of India and its associate banks via the CAMEL rating. Aspal and Malhotra (2013) and Lakhtaria (2013) have studied the financial performance of selected Indian public sector banks through the CAMEL rating model. Kumar et al. (2012) examined the performance of the top twelve highest market capitalized public and private banks in India with the help of CAMEL rating approach.

In our study we focus on the top five private sector banks by market capitalization and attempt to arrive at a ranking methodology for these banks based on the CAMEL approach. We simply don't rank the parameters as they are but rank the banks based on the five year CAGR of each of the CAMEL parameters.

2.0 Literature Review

The profitability of a bank often a key measure of performance is predominantly driven by a series of internal and external factors. The internal determinants of bank profitability include but are not limited to bank size, capital, risk management procedures adopted, expenses, and diversification (Molyneux and Thornton, 1992); Goddard et al. (2004); Bodla and Verma, (2006). External determinants of bank profitability include both industry structural determinants such as market concentration, industry size and ownership, and macroeconomic determinants such as inflation, interest rates, money supply and Gross Domestic Product (GDP) (Athanasoglou et al., 2008; Chirwa, 2003).

Yet another key bench mark of performance is clearly the stock price performance. The stock prices of banks are influenced by several factors. These include but are not limited to changes in bank profitability (Chu and Lim, 1998), bank specific risks (Adenso-Diaz and Gascon, 1997), microeconomic factors such as net asset value per share, dividend percentage, and earnings per share (Uddin, 2009), changes in operating and cost efficiency (Beccalli et al., 2006) and earnings announcements (Seetharaman and Raj, 2011).

The CAMEL rating methodology takes a more holistic view of performance examining it from several vantage points. Sangmi and Nazir, 2010 examined the CAMEL ratings of Punjab national bank and Jammu and Kashmir Bankin India from 2001 to 2005. They found out that both the banks were financially sound as per the CAMEL framework. Misra and Aspal, 2013 compared State Bank of India and its associate banks through the CAMEL rating methodology. He found that State Bank of India had significantly lower CAMEL ratings than its smaller associate banks.

Aspal and Malhotra, 2013 studied the financial performance of selected midsized Indian public sector banks with theCAMEL rating model from 2007 to 2011. They found that bank of Baroda and Andhra bank had the highest CAMEL ratings. Lakhtaria, 2013 studied the top three largest public sector banks namelyState Bank of India (SBI),Bank of Baroda and Punjab National Bank (PNB) using the CAMEL model. He found that the Bank of Baroda had the highest CAMEL rank followed by PNB and SBI.

Kumar et al., 2012 studied the performance of the top 12 Indian private and public banks by market capitalization through the CAMEL rating approach between 2000 and 2011. They found that that private sector banks fared much better than their public counterparts. Jha and Hui, 2012 similarly found that private sector banks outperformed their public counterparts among a cross section of Nepalese commercial banks. Kaur (2010) studied public and private sector banks operating in India via the CAMEL approach over a seven year period from 2001 to 2007. Andhra Bank and State Bank of Patiala ranked as the best public sector bank while Jammu and Kashmir Bank was the best private sector bank.

3.0 Methodology

We focus on developing a ranking methodology for a sample of public sector banks based on the five year CAGR of CAMEL parameters. The five CAMEL parameters are as follows: C – Capital Adequacy; A – Asset Quality; M – Management Efficiency; E – Earnings quality; L – Liquidity.

Capital adequacy is a measure of how adequately capitalised a bank is in its ability to absorb any losses and meeting customer obligations. Two measures of capital adequacy considered in this study are: (i) Capital Adequacy Ratio; and (ii) Debt to Equity Ratio. *Asset quality* is a measure of the bank's financial health. Improving asset quality is often marked by strong financial performance. Two measures of asset quality considered in this study are: (i) % Net Non-Performing Assets to Total Advances; and (ii) % Total Investment to Total Assets. *Management efficiency* measures how capable top management is in managing its operations and getting the most out of its work force. Two measures of asset quality considered in this study are: (i) Profit per employee; and (ii) Business per employee. *Earnings quality* looks at how profitable the bank is and its ability to deliver superior returns on its asset base deployed. Two measures of earnings quality considered in this study are: (i) Earnings per share; and (ii) %Operating Profit to Average Working Funds. *Liquidity* looks at how well the firm manages and generates its cash to overcome any asset liability mismatches in the near term. Two measures of liquidity considered in this study are: (i) % Cash to total deposits; and (ii) % Investment to total deposits

The 5 year CAGR is calculated as:

CAGR = $\{[\text{Ending Value}/ \text{Beginning Value}]^{1/5} - 1\} \times 100$

The CAGR each of the above parameters is calculated a five year period from the financial year ending March 2012 to financial year ending March 2017. Ranking is done for each of these parameters based on the CAGR obtained. The average rank for each category is determined. An overall CAMEL rank is developed based on average rank of the CAGR's of each of the above parameters and is used to rate the banks. Data on all banks is obtained from the Capitaline database (www.capitaline.com). The following five banks are chosen for the study based on their asset base and market capitalization:

1) HDFC Bank (HDFC)
2) ICICI Bank (ICICI)
3) Kotak Mahindra Bank (Kotak)
4) Axis Bank (Axis)
5) IndusInd Bank (IndusInd)

4.0 Results

Table 1 provides the key bank metrics of the selected banks. Table 2 shows the capital adequacy ratio of the five banks studied over the last five years and the five year CAGR of the capital adequacy ratio. IndusInd bank has the highest CAGR of the capital adequacy ratio and is ranked 1. HDFC bank has the lowest CAGR of the capital adequacy ratio and is ranked 5. Table 3 shows the debt to equity ratio of the five banks studied over the last five years and the five year CAGR of the debt to equity ratio. IndusInd bank has the lowest CAGR of the debt to equity ratio and is ranked 1. ICICI bank has the highest CAGR of the debt to equity ratio and is ranked 5. Table 4 shows the %NPA of the five banks studied over the last five years and the five year CAGR of the %NPA. IndusInd bank has the lowest CAGR of the %NPA and is ranked 1. Axis bank has the highest CAGR of the %NPA and is ranked 5.

Table 1: Some Key Bank Metrics (Billion Rupees)

Bank	Market Cap	Net Interest Income	Net Profit	Total Assets
HDFC	4254	693	146	7088
ICICI	1860	542	98	7718
Kotak	1812	177	34	2146
Axis	1239	445	37	6015
IndusInd	891	144	29	1401

Source: moneycontrol.com as on 03/07/17

Table 2: Ranking as per the Capital Adequacy Ratio

Bank/Year	2016-17	2011-12	CAGR	Rank
HDFC	16.5	14.6	-2.42	5
ICICI	18.52	17.39	-1.25	4
Kotak	17.52	16.8	-0.84	3
Axis	13.66	14.95	1.82	2
IndusInd	13.85	15.31	2.02	1

Source: The Capitaline database

Table 3: Ranking as per the Debt to Equity Ratio

Bank/Year	2016-17	2011-12	CAGR	Rank
HDFC	10.29	8.66	-3.40	2
ICICI	6.85	6.72	-0.35	5
Kotak	7.23	6.77	-1.30	4
Axis	11.52	9.79	-3.21	3
IndusInd	11.15	7.65	-7.24	1

Source: The Capitaline database

Table 4: Ranking as per the % Net NPA to Net Advances

Bank/Year	2016-17	2011-12	CAGR	Rank
HDFC	0.2	0.33	10.53	2
ICICI	0.73	4.89	46.28	4
Kotak	0.61	1.26	15.61	3
Axis	0.25	2.11	53.20	5
IndusInd	0.27	0.39	7.63	1

Source: The Capitaline database

Table 5 shows the %total investment to total assets of the five banks studied over the last five years and the five year CAGR of the %Total investment to Total assets. HDFC bank has the highest CAGR of the %Total investment to Total assets and is ranked 1. Kotak Mahindra bank has the lowest CAGR of the %Total investment to Total assets and is ranked 5. Table 6 shows the Profit per employee of the five banks studied over the last five years and the five year CAGR of the Profit per employee. HDFC bank has the highest CAGR of the Profit per employee and is ranked 1. Axis bank has the lowest CAGR of the Profit per employee and is ranked 5.

Table 5: Ranking as per the %Total Investment to Total Assets

Bank/Year	2016-17	2011-12	CAGR	Rank
HDFC	28.84	24.82	-2.96	1
ICICI	32.60	20.84	-8.562	4
Kotak	32.84	20.99	-8.564	5
Axis	32.62	21.41	-8.08	3
IndusInd	25.27	20.54	-4.05	2

Source: The Capitaline database

Table 6: Ranking as per Profit per Employee (10M Rupees)

Bank/Year	2016-17	2011-12	CAGR	Rank
HDFC	0.08	0.16	14.86	1
ICICI	0.11	0.12	1.76	4
Kotak	0.09	0.11	4.10	2
Axis	0.14	0.07	-12.94	5
IndusInd	0.09	0.11	4.10	2

Source: The Capitaline database

Table 7 shows the business per employee of the five banks studied over the last five years and the five year CAGR of the business per employee. HDFC bank has the highest CAGR of business per employee and is ranked 1. Axis bank has the lowest CAGR of business per employee and is ranked 5. Table 8 shows the % operating profit to average working funds of the five banks studied over the last five years and the five year CAGR of % operating profit to average working funds. ICICI bank has the highest CAGR of % operating profit to average working funds and is ranked 1. HDFC bank has the lowest CAGR of % operating profit to average working funds and is ranked 5.

Table 7: Ranking as per Business per Employee (10M Rupees)

Bank/Year	2016-17	2011-12	CAGR	Rank
HDFC	6.54	12.36	13.58	1
ICICI	7.08	9.89	6.91	2
Kotak	6.13	8.35	6.38	3
Axis	12.76	14	1.87	5
IndusInd	7.88	9.16	3.06	4

Source: The Capitaline database

Table 8: Ranking as per the %Operating Profit to Average Working Funds

Bank/Year	2016-17	2011-12	CAGR	Rank
HDFC	3.22	3.32	0.61	5
ICICI	2.41	3.64	8.60	1
Kotak	2.79	3.03	1.66	3
Axis	2.94	3.11	1.13	4
IndusInd	2.69	3.54	5.65	2

Source: The Capitaline database

Table 9 shows the earnings per share of the five banks studied over the last five years and the five year CAGR of earnings per share. IndusInd bank has the highest CAGR of earnings per share and is ranked 1. Axis bank has the lowest CAGR of earnings per share and is ranked 5. Table 10 shows the %cash to total deposits of the five banks studied over the last five years and the five year CAGR %cash to total deposits. Axis bank has the highest CAGR of %cash to total deposits and is ranked 1. HDFC bank has the lowest CAGR of %cash to total deposits and is ranked 5. Table 11 shows the %investment to total deposits of the five banks studied over the last five years and the five year CAGR %Investment to total deposits. HDFC bank has the highest CAGR of

%investment to total deposits and is ranked 1. Kotak bank has the lowest CAGR of %investment to total deposits and is ranked 5.

Table 9: Ranking as per Earnings per Share

Bank/Year	2016-17	2011-12	CAGR	Rank
HDFC	21.32	56.78	21.64	2
ICICI	9.85	15.29	9.19	4
Kotak	7.28	18.41	20.39	3
Axis	20.01	15.36	-5.15	5
IndusInd	16.8	47.95	23.34	1

Source: The Capitaline database

Table 10: Ranking as per the %Cash to Total Deposits

Bank/Year	2016-17	2011-12	CAGR	Rank
HDFC	8.81	5.71	-8.31	5
ICICI	8.6	6.45	-5.59	4
Kotak	6.08	4.86	-4.38	3
Axis	6.01	6.89	2.77	1
IndusInd	6.99	5.59	-4.37	2

Source: The Capitaline database

Table 11: Ranking as per the %Investment to Total Deposits

Bank/Year	2016-17	2011-12	CAGR	Rank
HDFC	36.99	34.48	-1.40	1
ICICI	61.16	35.32	-10.40	4
Kotak	57.06	32.54	-10.62	5
Axis	40.35	33.7	-3.54	3
IndusInd	36.65	32.22	-2.54	2

Source: The Capitaline database

Table 12 shows the individual segment ranks obtained by taking the average of the ranks of the two ratios that represent each segment and the overall CAMEL rank obtained by taking the average rank of each of the CAMEL segments. IndusInd bank was the best bank in terms of capital adequacy and earnings quality. IndusInd bank also ranked joint first with HDFC bank in asset quality and with Axis bank in liquidity.

HDFC bank ranked first in management efficiency. IndusInd bank achieved the highest overall CAMEL rank.

Table 12: Individual Segment and Overall CAMEL Rank

Bank	C	A	M	E	L	Overall
HDFC	3	1	1	4	3	2
ICICI	5	3	3	2	4	5
Kotak	3	3	2	3	4	3
Axis	2	3	5	5	1	4
IndusInd	1	1	3	1	1	1

5.0 Discussion and Analysis

We compare and rank the top five private sector banks by market capitalization in India via the CAMEL rating methodology. While studies on the CAMEL rating tend to focus on an average rank over a period of time we focus on developing a rank based on the CAGR of CAMEL parameters. This approach gives a better measure of performance given the tremendous change in the banking landscape in India over the last few years with reference to asset quality issues and the gradual implementation of Basel III norms by the RBI.

The top five private banks HDFC bank, ICICI bank, Kotak Mahindra bank, Axis bank and IndusInd bank were chosen based on their market capitalization (Table 1). The banks were ranked for the CAGR of each of the CAMEL parameters. The capital adequacy rank (Table 12) was estimated from the average of the ranks from the two sub categories the capital adequacy ratio (Table 2) and the debt to equity ratio (Table 3). IndusInd bank ranked first in capital adequacy while ICICI bank ranked last. Capital adequacy is a very useful metric and in a recent study Zarrouk et al., 2016 found that bank profitability in the Middle East and North Africa (MENA) region was positively affected by the level of capitalization.

The asset quality rank (Table 12) was estimated from the average of the ranks from the two sub categories the %NPA (Table 4) and the %total investment to total assets (Table 5). IndusInd bank and HDFC bank ranked joint first in asset quality followed by the other banks. Asset quality often has a direct bearing on profitability. In a recent study that involved U.S. regional banks during the period from 1994 to 2011, Growe et al., (2014) found that provisions for credit losses negatively impact profitability. The management efficiency rank (Table 12) was estimated from the average of the ranks from the two sub categories the profit per employee (Table 6) and business per employee (Table 7). HDFC bank ranked first in management efficiency while Axis bank ranked last. Management efficiency is a useful metric to consider in evaluating the efficiency of management and employees and Ben Naceur and Goaied, (2001) found that the best performing Tunisian banks are those that improve labor and capital productivity.

The earnings quality rank (Table 12) was estimated from the average of the ranks from the two sub categories the % operating income to average working funds (Table 8) and earnings per share (Table 9). IndusInd bank ranked first in earnings quality while Axis bank ranked last. Earnings quality is often an important barometer of stock price performance. Seetharaman and Raj, 2011 found a very strong positive correlation between earnings per share and the share price of a Malaysian bank. The liquidity rank (Table 12) was estimated from the average of the ranks from the two sub categories the % cash to total deposits (Table 10) and % investment to total deposits (Table 11). IndusInd bank and Axis bank ranked joint first in liquidity while ICICI bank and Kotak Mahindra bank ranked joint last.

The best overall CAMEL rank was obtained by IndusInd bank which was obtained from the average ranks of each one of the CAMEL parameters. However even IndusInd bank lagged behind in management efficiency. Management at IndusInd bank can focus on this area to strengthen IndusInd bank's position further. The other banks chosen in the study are lagging behind in several of the key CAMEL parameters and management can work on these areas to catch up with the leader IndusInd bank. Investors can look at CAMEL ratings and compare one bank to the other in their efforts to identify the best banks. The use of CAGR in the ranking process makes it more reflective of the banks performance over time.

6.0 Conclusion

We develop a ranking methodology based on the CAMEL rating system to compare the top five private sector banks by market capitalization. Out of the five banks chosen for the study IndusInd bank ranked first in capital adequacy and earnings quality. IndusInd bank also ranked joint first in asset quality with HDFC bank and joint first in liquidity with Axis bank. HDFC bank ranked first in management efficiency. The bank with the best overall CAMEL rank proved to be IndusInd bank. The incorporation of CAGR in the ranking process makes the rating more representative of actual performance. The CAMEL rating can serve as a useful measure to compare the performance of banks and can provide valuable insight to managers, investors, regulators and other stake holders of banks.

References

Adenso-Diaz, B. & Gascon, F. (1997). Linking and weighting efficiency estimates with stock performance in banking firms. *Wharton School Working Paper*, 97/21.

Aspal, P. K. & Malhotra, N. (2013). Performance appraisal of Indian public sector banks. *World Journal of Social Sciences*, 3(3), 71-88.

Athanasoglou, P.P., Brissimis, S.N. & Delis, M.D. (2008). Bank-specific, industry-specific and macroeconomic determinants of bank profitability. *Journal of International Financial Markets, Institutions & Money*, 18(2), 121-136.

Beccalli, E., Casu, B. & Girardone, C. (2006), Efficiency and stock performance in European banking. *Journal of Business Finance and Accounting*, 33, 245–262.

Ben Naceur S. & M. Goaied. (2001). The determinants of the Tunisian deposit banks Performance. *Applied Financial Economics*, 11, 317-19.

Bodla, B.S. & Verma, R. (2006). Determinants of profitability of banks in India: A multivariate analysis. *Journal of Services Research*, 6(2), 75-89.

Chirwa, E. W. (2003). Determinants of commercial banks profitability in Malawi: A co integration approach. *Applied Financial Economics*, 13(8), 565-571.

Chu, S.F. & Lim, G.H. (1998). Share performance and profit efficiency of banks in an oligopolistic market: Evidence from Singapore. *Journal of Multinational Financial Management*, 8, 155–68.

Goddard, J., P. Molyneux, & Wilson, J.O.S. (2004). The profitability of European banks: A cross-sectional and dynamic panel analysis. *Manchester School*, 72(3), 363-381.

Growe , G., M. DeBruine , J. Y. L. & Maldonado, J. F. T. (2014). The profitability and performance measurement of U.S. regional banks using the predictive focus of the fundamental analysis research. *Advances in Management Accounting*. 24, 189 – 237.

Jha, S. & Hui, X. (2012). A comparison of financial performance of commercial banks: A case study of Nepal. *African Journal of Business Management*, 6(25), 7601-11.

Kaur, H. V. (2010). Analysis of banks in India--A CAMEL approach. *Global Business Review*, 11(2), 257–280.

Kumar, M. A., Harsha, G. S., Anand, S., & Dhruva, N. R. (2012). Analyzing soundness in Indian banking: A CAMEL approach. *Research Journal of Management Sciences*, 1(3), 9–14.

Lakhtaria, N. J. (2013). A comparative study of the selected public sector banks through CAMEL model. *Indian Journal of Research*, 2(4), 37-38.

Misra, S. K., & Aspal, P. K. (2013). A CAMEL model analysis of State Bank group. *World Journal of Social Sciences*, 3(4), 36–55.

Molyneux, P. & Thornton, J. (1992). Determinants of European bank profitability: A note. *Journal of Banking and Finance*, 16(6), 1173-1178.

Sangmi, M. D. & Nazir, T. (2010). Analyzing financial performance of commercial banks in India: Application of CAMEL model. *Pakistan Journal of Commerce and Social Sciences*, 4 (1): 40-55.

Seetharaman, A. & Raj, J.R. (2011). An empirical study on the impact of earnings per share on stock prices of a listed bank in Malaysia. *International Journal of Applied Economics and Finance,* 5(2): 114-126.

Uddin, M.B. (2009). Determinants of market price of stock: A study on bank leasing and insurance companies of Bangladesh. *Journal of Modern. Accounting and Auditing*. 5(7), 1-7.

Zarrouk, H., Jedidia, K. B., & Moualhi, M. (2016). Is Islamic bank profitability driven by same forces as conventional banks? *International Journal of Islamic and Middle Eastern Finance and Management*, 9(1), 46–66.

YOUR KNOWLEDGE HAS VALUE

- We will publish your bachelor's and master's thesis, essays and papers

- Your own eBook and book - sold worldwide in all relevant shops

- Earn money with each sale

Upload your text at www.GRIN.com
and publish for free

www.ingramcontent.com/pod-product-compliance
Lightning Source LLC
LaVergne TN
LVHW041912070526
838199LV00051BA/2596